Advance praise {

MW00478160

"Powerful and brave, Anna C. Martinez's poetic memoir, *Pura Puta*, pulses with the electricity of a million beating hearts. Moving between the visceral and delicate, these poems are healing and transformative. What a badass Chicana poet."

—**Kali Fajardo-Anstine**, author of *Woman of Light* and American Book Award winner *Sabrina & Corina*

"This collection of poems by Anna Martinez achieves, on so many levels, what so many other practitioners are in hot pursuit of—mainly, poems sourced from the deepest refuges of the heart and soul that spill over the page like ancient tribal love songs, war songs, heroic in their tone and righteous in their claims, with a fluid style that's easy to read and challenging only in its idea to shatter boring convention so many poets rely on in fear of criticism—she is fearless, and every high school teacher needs to study these in class, college kids need to recite these in their reading circles and book clubs— go after your education, these poems will incite your intelligence, wake it up, and open your eyes as well as your heart!"

—**Jimmy Santiago Baca**, author of *A Place to Stand* and *When I Walk Through That Door, I Am*

"Here is a poetry collection concocted with electric words, stories of storm, rage, and infinite faith. Martinez's poetry is a prayer without repentance and she allows truth to be her ultimate spiritual guide. She weaves a poetic quilt stitched with her own special kind of medicine, which is to say, they are pieced together with the fabric of her ululating personal histories, traumas, and triumphs. It is an urgent, sharp collection of elegies to be read aloud and in the quietude of one's most intimate spaces. *Pura Puta* is both subtly soft and raucously loud as a deafening bomb. This collection will shout, sing, soothe, and assail your senses in the best possible way. Martinez does not disappoint. Prepare yourselves, readers, for a most fantastic literary journey."

–**Jessica Helen Lopez**, author of *The Blood Poems*
and City of Albuquerque Poet Laureate Emerita

"Martinez has crafted a beautiful collection full of magic found within the rough edges of the concrete reality she paints with her pen. Stories of family, perseverance, of the incredible strength of women across the vast expanse of this timeline. A portrait of her own strength to speak uncomfortable truths poetically to the patriarchy, mixed with the light glimmer of hope that can only be found in the sky of a northern New Mexico night. I was changed by this reading; it is a journey I would recommend to anyone with a beating heart."

–**Dylan Collins**, author of *In Our Hearts
Slowly Built a Thunder*

To Kent,
Thank you for
sharing this moment
w/ me

All my love
Pura

4/28/22

PURA PUTA

PURA PUTA

a poetic memoir

Anna C. Martinez

Casa Urraca Press
ABIQUIU

Set in Semplicita Pro and Arno Pro.
Author photograph by Adam Rubenstein.

25 24 23 22   1 2 3 4 5 6 7

First edition

Paperback ISBN 978-1-956375-03-9
Exclusive hardover ISBN 978-1-956375-10-7

CASA URRACA PRESS

an imprint of Casa Urraca, Ltd.
PO Box 1119
Abiquiu, New Mexico 87510
casaurracapress.com

To Lucy and Andrés,
Lougardita and Fedelina.

POEMS

I write because life does not appease my appetites and hunger.

—Gloria Anzaldúa

PÍNCHE MALINCHE LLORONA
EATER of DEATH
COATLICUE (or, HOW IT BEGAN)

Oye aztec warrior
once there was and
once there was not.

Don't need your arms no more
attached to your fist
attached to your prick
attached to your hypocrite
as if any Aztlán exists that didn't first burst her hips
lips
you stitch
whore
myth
while she chops your wood and suckles your seed
as if she not forge-tempered in your fucking pyre
honed
ground in sparks against your head
kicking screaming broken in your bed
bound gagged silent like you like her, *no?*
erotic
as is to you
beauty sexy goddess
draped helpless in your arms she turns you on emplumado
hard
proud
exotic
fresh meat throbbing pink inexperience sobbing innocence

preferred desired required commodity in your lust trade
reaming impaling her from behind and inside out and
          without pause the same to her skull
call her *whore*
fuckhole
drowned in your blown load
thrown over your shoulder carried in offering to your
          friends and brothers
adorned in necklace of her nipples
trod up mountain of her skull to temple of her sacrifice
          at altar of the world and
had she known
she'd have been satisfied as myth
asswipe
instead of *beautysexysultrygoddessprincesshead* now
          branded again
instigator of your pínche war
goddess of your mierda
your desmadre
your malinche llorona
hollowed eyes echo inside wonder why you first
          decapitate her, *no?*
castrate her
chop her to pieces
feed to the same
obsidian rip her open gullet to womb

excise her magic
assuage your fear
sever her of weapon she wields stronger than any
        you will ever know
own
feel
its beat
makes you stop
finally stop
her blood drips hot from your hand until
still it stands
scrape her name from trees
temples
pyramids of the sun
promised lands undone in absolute power wielded
no drop of blood yielded in your skull mountain
        climbs to gold
vision
more virgins
but her placenta dripping scrambling stars burrowing
        into your killing field warrior
a donde naciste por su sangre
a donde nunca hallaras descanso por ser tragado
        de sus gusanos
burrowing memory into your killing field warrior
llevandose con ella las flores la fruta el río

your fate is sealed
renascida entre ella misma de la ceniza
I will claw my way up
out behind steal yours in the night,
drag them down to the river and hold them under
so cry to the motherfucking wind like you made mine
mama/abuela/hija/hermanita/nieta
as slithering coiled fangs talons
myth
all the better to eat you with motherfucker
swallowed whole and headfirst like you like
your only chance at myth and
only when and if
I spit you back
as once there was and
once there was not.

SOY CHICANA

Por siempre y mal me has pintado de tu vestido de aguantar
telado de listón azul, negro, morado como mis labios
por bien de tus ojos y macho
Tan pesado
fatal
destiñido como los años
manchada por sangre de mi alma fiel que
lla ni se limpia de mis manos.
Sera cierta que lla no aguanto estas cintas antiguas
        que aprietan mi ser
Creelo
Veelo
que me salgo desnuda
sin vergiienza ni lagrimas
corriendo por el campo a gritar y liberarme al fin de tu
        pínche aguantar.

Ves que soy Chicana
de Fuego
Viento
Mar soy
Chicana
de pelo negro
cafe los ojos
passiones rojos soy
Chicana

Soñando
Tomando
ahogando soy
Chicana
Virgen
Malinche
Tonantzin soy
Chicana
Despreciada
Olvidada
liberada soy
Chicana
de pasado robado
presente dado
futuro reclamado soy
Chicana de piedra seda y tierra
y pescenme
si de verdad pueden.

ESCAPE

as born to a pair of self-proclaimed river rats
then living in an L.A. apartment with a pool
chosen to sea legs
soon as I was let go in the shallow end by my mom
to see what I would do
and I just did
let loose at three months old
dived and bobbed as if I had fins
months before my chubby feet ever touched ground
in corrective leather high tops
mom would swear I'd wear them
as they'd paid a hundred bucks for them
you're so clumsy you trip on lines in the sidewalk
trip over your own shadow
she'd tease then twist them onto my kicking feet
my first memory
her and my first fight
three years old
over ugly shoes I learned quickly to untie
first of daily barefooted fights
followed us back from the singe of Manhattan Beach
        sidewalk and sands
to the sticky black river mud layers of home

naturally my favorite escape growing up
from the misery of summer

was to back-float in the waters of the Río
eyes closed
elbows bent
fingers interwoven
palms cradled my head
feet crossed
toes wiggled above the surface
ears flooded tranquil
green water echoed my breath
hhuh-haaa
hhhhuuh-haaaa
squinted my eyes open every once in a while to
reckon distance between me and that whirlpool
     swirled midway across
rolled by beach waves before
they usually spit you back to shore
but that whirlpool
tried my best to keep my eye and keep amused
     by the canopy of cottonwood trees
spaded leaves
shaded and winked
sunlight glam silver lash leaves
shade for my peace
unlike giggles and splashes from sisters playing
     shark hunt in knee deep water and
caution grito every once in a while

from mom and the grownups drinking beer on the shore
hhuuuh-haaa
I wondered what lurked beneath
snakes
I'd seen them scouring undergrowth
dark network of roots and burrows
exposed where the bank had given way
fish
not pretty little princess iridescent state fish rainbow trout
eaten straight from the campfire
but pike
dinosaur fish
four feet long with teeth like needles
carp
sucker fish with long slimy mustaches
tickled like haunted fingers reaching for the sunlit surface
haunting my daydreaming brain
a rotting corpse weighed down by a tree branch
nibbled on by cute little fish
playing out scenes on eyelid mini screens
too loud for my ears to pick up
mom yell as
whirlpool grabbed me
again
spun me
sucked me under

spat me back as I gasped for air
dogpaddled
to the wrong side of the river
where laughter knew no bounds.

THE HARVEST
(in Six Parts)

space occupied by the oldest girl child
in a family with kids
is a corn maze
borderland between child and mom
caregiver
blame
and *swallow those tears*
assumed to be strong enough
to care for herself
that part never goes away

my dad an artist
my mom a seamstress
songstress
modeled for one
posed for the other
can't sing worth a damn
only things I knew I was good at were
reading aloud and
being looked at

I found places to hide
to read in the silence
a collector of stories
my borderland
a library

dismembered recollections gathered from the shadows
heard from around the corner
where I was supposed to have been asleep
stories repainted through the palate of
each telling's taste and each teller's tongue
retold in the gray
then remembered again that way

I.
grandma was the cosecha
big family woman
mom's mom Lougardita
grandma Lou
or just Lou
but grandma to me
back bent at the waist
eyes closed to a slant
fingers picking chile
plant to plant
row to row
straw hat shone rays so huge the sun must've surely noticed
as sweat ran down between those gallon-jug chíches
adobe
color of home
of acequias run
row to row
barbed-wire fence to barbed-wire fence
century to century and still

where now her eight daughters
know the path at night
over the acequia through the barbed wire fence
        to Tía Bita's house
each time he gets home dragging dusty shoes
muttering spit to himself

half-spoken words on repeat
a beat she knew
but her girls got away
she gives thanks to god
while she ran circles from him
around the kitchen table
long enough to tire his awake
escapes with only her nalga slashed
after he'd grabbed the very knife from the cutting board
bloodied from the carnitas she had just cut and cooked
     for him
and slashed at her
frustrated he couldn't catch her

blood running
acequia down her leg
they carried him to bed
her to the kitchen tabletop where she lay
Ave Maria Purisima
ass up
butt cheek slit open
panties pulled down
in full sight
kids seen her as they'd never seen
but now they'll not forget
nor will she

this thing she will never confess
never see that tabletop the same
nor the dress
nor spare breath for the shame crushing her top-heavy breasts
to the acrylic tabletop
only because she could not reach around to stitch it herself

her young son
stitches it closed
with needle and thread
in unsteady hand
cleans the blood with a dish towel cut from a Pansy flour sack
acts as if she doesn't feel
the thread being pulled
the weight
the sting
the prayer
the shame
the tremble of her son's hand
the tug
the thread
the son that would never leave home again

II.

first day of fall
first day of my sister's life
first grown up shower
I was used to taking baths
sometimes grandmas do things differently
grandpas too

grandma was all busy
getting ready for a new baby
cooking cleaning
in and out of the house
hanging clothes on the line
took me to the shower in the bathroom in my mama's room
turned on the water
quickly pulled up my dress
hands up right over my head
left the panties for me to do when she's gone
a tiny grown-up bathroom
white tile and cold
I crossed my arms hands tucked in my armpits
grandma said she'd be right back to shampoo my hair

tiny shower was like a closet
I closed my eyes to the small space
always been scared of being closed in

I turned my back to the water
sang a song I knew from my heart
to the raining inside my head
shampooed my own hair
for grandma to see
the door clicked open as I rinsed
couldn't keep in my grin
soon as I knew the suds were all out
I opened my mouth to say
words that stuck frozen in my throat

why grandpa
grandma's getting me out
I say or think
I don't know
he puts his finger to his lips
then to mine
then between mine
wraps me in the towel
leaves the water running
carries me to mama's bed
always careful with me
always smells so good and sweet
like he's going someplace
or been someplace

don't worry I'm gonna make you all pretty
careful when he lays me down
careful when he opens the towel

grandma out the window hanging sheets
      on the backyard line
I just can't believe
wish to god mom would have the baby soon
wish to god she'll have a boy

III.

summer wakes slowly on grandma Lou's farm
light pools and stirs me
on the squeaky metal frame bed
tucked in the corner of the living room
behind the squeaky leather lazy boy chair
in the center of the room with the best view
        of the westerns on TV
the chair each one of us would vacate when grandpa
        walked in
grandpa in his chair
smelling sweet
watching TV
bathed in its blue essence
a calming dull reflected in his eyes
a safe memory for all
for after all
I did love him
always careful with me
always conflicted me
a sin I still seem to wear on my sleeve
or my chest
or my back
no matter how leathery red our skin can get
some of us still have blue eyes
looking back
it was the clock that woke me

blue-eyed Jesus of the Sacred Heart with heavy hands
tick tock that stuck at certain times
click/click/clicks
until it pushed past minute by minute
clicking and ticking in my head
had to rub the sun wash from my eyes
bacon gets me up
barefooted on a floor that changes from room to room
warming brown patchwork linoleum
to pale yellow tile in the room with the books
grandma's books
untouched
all the great stories I'd ever heard about
my haven
in a home that required the work of all its residents
three mixed families
two dozen mouths to feed
at least
a chore for everyone
and grandma said my work was to read
nobody else liked that

ceramic cold to my bare feet
reminded me I was in the kitchen
la cocina
where grandma stands at the wood stove

silver curls wrapped in a blue paño
mirror premonition of the now-silver me
(save for my 40DDS
no comparison to her triple O-GGG chichis
hung loose to her knees at the drop of her bra
bitch please
so would yours after suckling fourteen babies on them things)
even the same
square hands
clap and toss tortillas
slapped onto the woodstove top
next to the two-story coffeepot

sientate
she says and I do
she turns down the radio that
looks like Professor's on Gilligan's island
daily obituaries sponsored by Block's Mortuary
thanks to god
nobody we know this morning

she unwraps the stack of steaming tortillas
smears one with butter
folds it in half and hands it to me
I smile as there is nothing I have to share
no matter how much I eat

soon there's a new pile
soon after there's three
down to the last ball of dough
she's saved for me
quieres rolar la ultima, mi'jita?
you want it to roll the last one?
she rolls the ball in her hand
smashes it to the countertop
mmm hmm I nod quickly
ven
the pin smaller than my mom's
rolls smoothly under my square hands
a white tongue of dough
she watches over my shoulder
like this?
closes arms around me to stretch it out
aver
looks like una mapa de Africa
pero who cares
it won't come rolling in
bring it pa' l'estufa
I peel it up
it shifts shapes in my hand
droops to a valentine heart
with a hole pulling through and getting bigger
aye nonononono

that's how you hang shortes from the percha
not carry tortilla to the stove
hací mira
she claps the dough from one hand to the other
easy fix
this one will be for your daddy she says

IV.
dad's mom Fedelina
grew an oasis
on her little plot in the
concrete Los Angeles block
at the corner of Rosecrans Boulevard and
      Inglewood Avenue
where thick angry power lines strung through
      transformer fists
thrummed in swags overhead

pink roses
gardenias
sun-kissed daisies
sugar lilacs
towering hollyhocks
all swayed to the buzz of honeybees
her home a tiny white cottage with a white picket fence
misfit planted in the midst of cinderblock wrought-iron-
      bar city

a lifetime away
from dark northern New Mexico nights
in Arroyo del Agua
where she spent her youth on a mountaintop
waiting for my grandfather

I never knew him
nor did my dad really know
this shepherd
teacher
after whom he was named Andrés
who passed at age forty-nine
six days before my dad's tenth birthday
3/12/51

nobody is sure how he met Fedelina
but they are sure he did not ask for her hand in marriage
until she had suffered six pregnancies of his
without him
buried three babies
before they were even weaned

story goes
her oldest brother Juan
threatened to kill Andrés with his bare hands
if he did not marry her
still he did not propose
instead at age thirty-five
he rode buckboard over the hills of Arroyo del Agua
porcelain mother at his side
on his way to propose to a way-too-young girl
only to find she was promised to another

he finally proposed to Fedelina
who after years of deliberation in the dark
expressed the conditions of their matrimonio
get me down off this mountain
near the church
where my children can learn
so he bought her a house in Santa Cruz de la Cañada
my dad was the first child born of the legal marriage
hates being called Junior
only memory he has of his dad
is riding early morning dark in his pickup truck
they stop and park
where his dad says *I'll be right out*
lie down on that seat until I come back
or something to that effect
in Spanish
more than an hour passed
dad finally peeked to see where they were at
the only café they knew
grandpa loved biscuits and gravy
had to fill his belly
for the long trip to the hills
where he would drop off his young sons
left with a couple cans of potted meat
for what must have been a week
to watch over the sheep

while he went to town for his business
leaving this as the myth
his sons would carry of him

years down the line Fedelina packs her life
leaves her home to the elements
to follow her kids as they graduate and migrate to Califas

V.

a generation later
Fedelina loved the city
its distractions
as did I
as I rode to her house one day
a month shy of twelve years old
the summer I started to bleed was when I was
first almost taken by a predator on the street
nearly plucked from a borrowed cruiser bike
told auntie a lie that I was only going to circle the block
really hoping to reach
Manhattan Beach
in theory three manageable major-street stretches
I memorized in reverse
as we returned from the beach one day
Manhattan Beach Boulevard to Hawthorne Boulevard
Hawthorne to
Rosecrans to
Prairie to
Lemoli to
West 135th, 134th Street
3252
six miles
I had no clue

an afternoon of
East L.A. mural tour for mom and dad
was my big chance
no trouble convincing my aunt of my lie
off I went on her otherwise-never-used beach cruiser
pedaling down the street
I began to think how absolutely no one knew
where I was or where I was headed
but I shrugged it off until

a block from grandma's house
at a red light
a Plymouth Fury rumbled on the street next to me
looked so much like my dad's silver blue Satellite
Plymouth
I peeked side-eyed at the man at the wheel
older than my dad
dark skinned
not black or Chicano
panama hat
tried not to look back
but he saw me see him
or I saw him see me but whatever
light turned green
nothing more to see

but I did think
stopping at grandma's might be a good
drink-of-water break
alibi bait
okay

I pedaled that way
for a moment forgetting about the Fury
until I see
he has kept up with me
or me with him
as I see the cars backed up behind
some honking their horns I think
all I can see is
he keeps keeping up with me
as I pedal my feet to a blur
keeps me framed in the side mirror
all the way to grandma's house
where I turn in
hoping he noticed me not noticing him

she wasn't home
I rode to the back yard and sat
waited in all of the shade of a tiny tree
grew both lemons and limes
waited

ate a lime from the tree
waited
ten minutes
twenty
stood up
shook the blood flowing sparks from my leg
watched grass stretching back toward the sun
in a fallen space shaped like my ass
opened the gate and rode around the corner
the Fury had waited
and had renewed the chase
no time
I knew a park three blocks away
all I could hope was to lose him
but he looked right at me
I stood up
pumped the pedals with all my thunder thigh
bike swayed left right left right left right
Fury kept up
leftright leftright leftright
careen down the sidewalk
ramp curbs
dodge pedestrians
run a red light
so does the Fury
lefrightlefrightlefright

pedals can't keep up
lose my footing
pedals spin
without me
almost fall
don't cry
green light
fuck
sweat in my eyes
sides ache
breathe
I'm not fast enough
breathe
I won't make it
breathe I can't breathe I can't I can't I can't god help
please I can't   breathe
down an alley
all went black and white
Fury zoomed around the corner
would be close
oh god
too close
too late
the Fury's twisted grin feet ahead at the end of the alley
back car door held open like a grave
he waited out of sight

in shiny polyester shirt
creased pants
shiny shoes that tapped as he moved
I slammed on the brakes
bike skidded out from under me
open car door grinned inches from my face
smell of burnt rubber broadcasting my fate but
he threw his arms around the nothing I left as I fell
slipped his grip from my ponytail clip
fingers brushed the back of my tee
he chased
feet tapping
I raced through a walkway gate to my old school
ditched the bike and ran
crouched in the door well of my old classroom
swallowed by the shadows
willing myself flat to the wall
his shoes tapping
closing in tapping
kicked at the ditched bike tapping
away in a cloud of curses to the open-mouth Fury tapping
I waited
prayed
to live and try another day
waited
waited

waited
waited
fought the instinct to look around the turn
waited
waited
after a certain amount of silence
a minute or an hour I could not say
finally stood up and rode away
left right, left right, left right
did not dare look back
did not ever tell

VI .

we never had rain like that before
mom had just saved enough for new carpeting
new furniture
new wooden bunk beds
after a life of sleeping four sisters in one full-sized bed
rain that would not stop
slowly formed a pond at the top of the driveway
pond gave way
slithered down the driveway
recollected outside the living room door
mom and I waded into the cold rains
shoveled in vain
all the runoff from the neighborhood
including the massive Catholic church next door
cast its shadow upon our yard
flooded the low-lying land of our home
we dug and dug to reroute
to no avail
dark booming skies promised more
we dropped shovel and ran inside
brand new carpet not yet tacked or glued
she and I rolled away from the door just in time
        to clear it a path
fingers of stream
creeping through the tiny space under the door
spilling like horizontal moonrise

spilling shine across the floor
mom cried
I'd never seen her tears before
we both cried
the sky crashed
power went out
my brother and sisters huddled top bunk
watched the water rise outside our window
hurry let's pray
mom said
grabbed our hands in circle
she and I leaned on my bed as
thunder mocked
hail beat down
lightning flashed
newly painted walls
mama sobbed the first set
OurFatherHailMaryGloryBe
begged the second
ourfatherhailmaryglorybe
scolded the third
OURFATHERHAILMARYGLORYBE and
roof stopped rattling and
somebody must've heard because
dark sky parted
waters backed off

without touching the new carpet
sunlight glistened from drifts of hailstones
anchoring the walls outside
mom had run off a storm
and continued with her day
as if nothing had happened

she had a dream that night
that my baby sister had been taken from her bed
and in that dream god parted the skies
in an angry voice said to her
that now she had a reason to cry
and I didn't understand
the goddamned shame god expected her to have

THREE MYSTERIES

the first bedtime story I remember
came from my dad
who attended art school during the day
watched us at night
mom worked swing shift
on the make-up assembly line at Max Factor
(fools put her on the line rather than the cover)
mom taught me to read but
dad kept me supplied with
books from his school library
and later
with a ten-dollar bill in pocket
for every book fair day
ten dollars
a lot for a kid from a family of seven
ten dollars was all there was left sometimes
after paying bills
from dad's biweekly post office check
all that was left to get us to the next
as I'd overheard late-at-night discussions in bed
no te apenes, babe
god always provides

the story he told me that night
story of a father and son

came from the one book on his shelf that I was denied
        access to
book I most longed to hold all by myself
thickest book in the house
one bordered in gold
sat on the highest shelf
he brought down one night
to settle me down
she could be so smart, but she has her head in the clouds

although I'd never seen the inside
knew the book soon as he began
flipped through to the story he wanted to read
couldn't understand why they'd kept it from me
every picture in that forbidden book
was a painting I already knew
from the time I spent inside
the art books on the lower shelves
that book
it was nothing new at all!
the nativity
story of his birth
told to me
more so than it was read
imagine

as god's son
he could have been born wherever he wanted
the highest mountain
most beautiful temple
castle
even Disneyland
dad laughed at what would have been my choice
his dad
trusted him enough to let him choose
and even though other people
might say it was stupid
he chose a stable
where everyone
and every beast
could celebrate him

a lesson in humility
registered instead
in my busy little head
as free will
the magic was in the decision
the ability to see
to know beyond the known
god
in my idle little hands

was mom gifted me salvation
through her own fear of hell
though she'd always been in god's good graces
there was a devil that sometimes escaped the reaches
      of her mind and
leapt right out into her dark corners
when she was alone
being the light
Lucia
had always attracted the dark
having always attracted the dark
she learned quickly to repel it with
a quick wave
sign of the cross
Ave Maria Purisima
invoking the Mother whose song she sings to start
      each day
before the morning light
one rosary per mile of her morning walk
a walk to keep herself in a borderland
between prediabetes and her one and only vice
wine
as if that were one
five decades a rosary
five rosaries a day
for five decades now

the joyful
the sorrowful
the glorious
the mystery

her turning point
the story of a child with her same name
that haunted her days
frightened into changing her ways
my mom's favorite story
Lucia of Fatima
who had been given a glimpse of the fires of hell
by the joyful sorrowful glorious Mother herself
Lady of Fatima
whose image graced the grotto
out front of my mom's parish named for the Baptist

I remembered that story because
Lucia of Fatima was asked to learn to read and write
so she could carry the message of the Mother
who caused the sun to dance
so all could believe
you'd better believe my mama believed
what I could not believe
what stuck me about that story
was that the Immaculate Heart

sorrowful Mother
would call Lucia Francisco and Jacinta
just kids
trying to play
to face the open pit of hell
as a warning
to secure their places in heaven
what the goddamned hell
if they had to give up everything good
to avoid the devil
shit
a curious kid like me
had a snowball's chance
little wiseass
too smart for your own good

Sofia was my mom's favorite girl's name
Sofia
she would have named herself
Wisdom
the mother of light
Lucia
name she wished she'd have passed on to me
instead she taught me to read by the time I was three
so I could believe for myself
I believed

believed I had real issues with the idea of forever
to any eternity
burning
believed I could negotiate for myself
not with her god
but his human son
a deal where he would just thump me on the head instead
whenever he saw me headed in that general hell direction
like any good father should
because I knew even as a girl
I could never remain unstained
it only takes one stain
to keep you out
as I was already tainted
scarlet
as is the nature of a girl
according to the god of Lucia

didn't realize then that I'd exchanged
eternal hellfire for
alternative hell on earth of
instant karma
and it burns
collected in full
one sinful act at a time
as sin is the nature of girl

its vessel
as man is the image of god
men forgive the sins of men but
the sin of a girl is blood
bloodstain does not erase
slippery slope to hell
for an articulate girl
thought I had no choice
vowed to silence
invisibility
only way for woman to attain humility
humanity
divinity
love
union
thought of becoming a nun
like Lucia of Fatima
convinced it was the only way
until I bled
realized that for me the convent would only
increase my sin
not decrease

men usurping god
decide the purpose of woman
never fought off so many sexual advances

so many men
as I did as a girl
things I didn't think I could ever tell my dad
or my mom
try as you may to never get caught alone
sometimes you can't avoid being
molested in the dark
and when you can avoid it
usually means
someone else takes it for you
I never imagined that in the deafening darkness of it
some sins you just can't confess
or apologize for

I came not to bring peace, but a sword
said the lord
so I made a deal at the cross road in my head
on a prayer as I laid in bed
I'll take my hell here, thank you
served one sin at a time
an appeal to the kinder side of god
in his earth-bound human son
my own story became entangled in his net.

PERIOD POWER

my mom had a strong period
she was a substitute teacher and
one day in biology class
one hormonal boy whispered to another that
"wouldn't it be chingon to dale huelo a la Lucy"
wouldn't it be cool
to *give it* to my mom
now I knew she was on her period that day and
not taking Midol
or any crap like that for irritability but
she probably was wearing
four super Kotex all at once
the kind in the purple box
she would trick me into the store to buy
under giggle and guise that
I'd be buying ice cream sandwiches

I'd forget that ice cream sandwiches
was her code name for sanitary pads
until she laughed
as she handed me the cash
in that Piggly Wiggly parking lot
not only
would I not be getting chocolate,
I'd be getting the biggest most colorful box
        in the feminine hygiene aisle

I'd look left
right
make a beeline for those things
try to hide the box as I dragged it alongside my leg but
it was like a suitcase
with blooming roses

I'd get to the register
cashier said she thinks they're on sale
blew into the mic
announced a price check for those
hundred-thousand-count super Kotex
Vince Torrez
the most handsome guy at Española Valley High
would rush by
ask what color box
and how many
and wink and dash away

but behind me
line got longer and longer
my face redder and redder
I just wanted to pay regular price
get the hell out of there
but mom would know they were on sale
send me back

for change
or exchange and
I wanted to tap that mic and scream
they're not for me
I wear Tampax, regulars
ten count

mom would still be giggling
when I walked back to the car
haha
I'd laugh nervously back
over her four pads at a time
then pray
mine never gets that bad

way it had to have been
that day in biology class
when a boy wanted a piece of her ass
how with one hand she grabbed that boy
lifted him and the desk off the ground,
shook him around
dragged his ass to the door
shoved him into the hall and slammed that door shut

I become aware of a totally new concept that day
period power

force so strong
moves oceans and moons
synchronizing mothers, daughters, roommates, lovers
oh yeah
lovers
my old man didn't believe
don't even tell me that shit

but one day
I started my period
I caught him hiding in the bedroom closet
shoving my fancy Cadbury chocolate bar in his mouth
foil ripped to strips
caramel creamed his lips
eyes bulged in fear
that I'd want a piece
then
in fabulous realization
that I had been right.

CORRÍDO de LUCIA ALMA

my mom Lucia Alma
her name means "light of the soul"
and she is
and though we always wondered
mostly her
why she named me Anna Carol
instead of Anna Lucia
now I know
my name means
"I am god's joyful song"

(even though I could not carry a tune
just keep your day job mija dad would say)

as she is god's joyful song
and back in the day nothing lit up her soul
like Little Richard's real rock 'n' roll
y allí les va el corrído de Lucia

with a flip of her long sponge-roller curls
shining like licorice
and a smack of her always lipsticked lips
she flips through the pile
picks, smiles
slowly slips vinyl from its sleeve
caresses by the edges between palms

blows for old dust
holds at label
shines it on her sleeve
sets with reverence on the turntable platter
in a manner of sacrificial feast
to that music beast
Magnavox console stereo
whose dropped needle
always finds the wax smooth of the right groove
yet crackles from battle scars of
so many sunset to sunrise
Spañada drinking/spilling/45-flipping
spinning/twisting/cackling/smoking Spaña
        Saturday nights

que chulita te /lookin' out my/por lo mucho que te…
can't get no/color TV/'cause dialing for dollars/picked
        a fine time…

Lucy knew all the words
had to memorize first
toss her five kids outside
lock the door behind
too nice to be inside
pulls out her pad to write and write
memorize

sing it high
try it low
do it again
lower lip pinched white between her teeth
slips thumb under the stylus to lift
go back
slip into the right groove, verse
sing line for line
etched into her mind and
out the window recorded
for all of time in mine
in bass rumbles and treble tremors
Magnavox rocked the entire neighborhood
vecinos, escuela, plaza, morada, iglesia y convento
de la Villa Nueva de la Santa Cruz de la Cañada
as for now
she's got a plan
sends him out for another bottle of wine
and a six-pack of Cracker Jack
'cause I'd get two boxes to babysit
but I'd do it for free
just to get my hands on the
LPs and 45s tucked inside that
Magnavox stereo console beast
where she'd rack a stack of 45s,
post in front of the mirror before he arrived

in pink-can Aqua Net aerosol cloud
beehive came to life
styling
singing
Maybelline
false eyelashes
smacked lips garnet red
a "buzz-ard" going in her head
a knockout
known by guys for miles around
for her tiny waist and healthy thighs
but she's got her man
she just wanted to dance
all dolled up he don't stand a chance
once he's back
she insists
he's convinced
can't resist
as she held out her hand
to lift him off the couch for a bit of practice
hands on her waist
hers on his hips
bit her lip
steps one, two, chachacha
guided him
'cause he was watching his feet

one, two
chachacha

let's do it again

but hon
rolled his eyes
one, two
dropped her hand
chachacha
stomped her toe
but hon

but she's not through
pulled up her skirt
for a bit of slip to slip
dipped her knees
swayed her hips
let that dance-off begin

okay
so Mashed Potato then
do the Twist
the Swim
the Jerk
Hitchhike

Stroll
got to Pony like Bony Maroni
do the Watusi

she knew them all
his little Lucy
hell he couldn't help but grin
she'd do it again
they'd spin meet eye to eye
nose to nose
chin to chin
hip to hip
then lip to lip
just in time
for Friday night
at that dive at the end of Riverside Drive
      with the bright neon sign
calling out both Saints and Sinners.

CHIMAYÓ CHEVY PICKUP, STEP SIDE '69

she chuckled at his question-by-numbers
as she remembered them by
car/make/model
American mostly
Chevy
diamond-tucked leather
pleated overheated
heaved over the front bucket seat into the back
on her back
windshield beaded of breath excreted

root beer Bel Aire
ooh sexy eyes
revving high
racing stripe black-and-white Malibu tight
        checkerboard leather
she wonders whether this one will be back

blue Chevy pickup rumbling
fingers fumbling
steering column stick shift encumbering
static on the AM
hips bumping the knob
rolling back from Wolfman Jack to KRLA
sixteen candles
a thousand miles away she begs him stay
begs

low-low cigarette-pack-low Impala
candy-apple diamond-tucked
they both pretend to ignore the glamour shot
tucked in his driver-side visor
eyes her over
who's that lady
a flick of the finger switch
sends hydraulics hopping
she locking fingers around his neck
white leather to squeal the spread of her legs

blue Chevy pickup rumbling
fingers hovering over the phone
running through smoke swirling
from the red tip of the borrowed cigarette dangling
     off her lip
lifts the shade just in time to see
Chevy pull away
watches her feet chasing down
racing down
naked down the street
if leaving me is easy
wrapped in a bed sheet
chasing down taillights hoping for red
so much unsaid it's speak now or

Malibu
now driving silver plush interior wire-spoke wheels
dropped-to-the-floor '78 T-bird
loops around the old Sonic
where he'd said it once but his whispers touched just too much
but two years gone by
she didn't think twice to hop in his ride
cruised her through town showing her around
to his friends and their dart-away eyes and
she don't mind she don't mind she don't mind
running fingers through his hair touching him there
just to hear it said under his breath

coldassmetalshellwhiteSuburban
doublebarrelshotgunrack hollowedoutnoseatintheback
woolenhorseblanketthrownoverjaggedfloorboardcancerspots
and splinteredbitsofalfalfaandhay and
hick don't even try to say it

not colder though than black Camaro
down by the river to smoke a toke
together baby
he keeps pouring her Crown
she can't wait to pee
squats down beneath the monkey peanut tree
near the edge where

he shoves her in
head over panties
water washes over like WHATTHEFUCK
struggles up for air through
wet web of her hair
mid November
stabbing icicle air
she is pissed
pulling up Levi's
stumbling to shore
teeth rattling screaming battling
fucking dripping red river on his black leather
wondering whether she will come back

combats all but the blood-red
shackle of hickeys choking her throat
purple and blue five finger prints between her thighs
but she survives

funny
as she just hopped in that ride down Riverside Drive
so that he could see her pull away
as he sat parked and watching in
that pínche blue pickup Chevrolet

and she chuckles again remembering them
even the most recent
Hyundai gray
didn't make the cut but so what
a reminisce from red tip of freshly licked and rolled smoke
billows like rock 'n' roll dreams from her sun-faded Chevy van
where she vows that she still can
though young face fades
like legs do from tan to strong
best to keep your eyes on the road
best to slow this vehicle down
wine
plush
rotating recline captain's chairs
moonlight dances on her hair
like a vision
she will lay you there
rear continental spare
eight cylinder
8-track
player
runs fingers through her gray
jet black back in the day
and fuck yeah
that's alright with her.

ODE to CHOCOLATE

days late you show your face,
bearing gift proffered
only after debating nights
awake inside your head
contrive to temper me remembering
my good love
you set and slide your offer on the counter
I slide it back knowing damned well
you won't take *no*
you lift the box, slowly walk up behind,
loop your arms and hold the gift
an inch from my heaving
you breathing in my ear and
I melt
drip
then remember how you avoid me during that one week
every month of our year
drip
if I had my mom's blood magic I'd use it here to
will my blood into next week
try as I may
I drip and
say *what the hell*
take it while the oven's hot and all that and
I grab the box
strip the red ribbon

open wide
pluck one out
gently bite
the double-dipped flat bottom
hides a cherry inside that
I lick
lull
roll and
suck it
tuck it
between cheek and gum to save for last as
tip of tongue dips in pink cherry nougat
open wide
I sigh
lick it clean inside *oh my*
and crush the shell to chips
it creams my lips
lick them clean yeah
and *my fingers too oh yeah* and
I dig between cheek and gum
pluck that cherry in offer
to you on tip of tongue
'cause baby
that's all you're gonna get.

LABOR of LOVE

Christmas Eve
mom's table
chisme with my sisters as
we tie bows on thirty dozen tamales
I can hardly wait to have a hot one
first thing in the morning
I say
that's if you make it 'til morning
mom replies
scent of corn and chile swag the kitchen air
their lifeblood stains my hands
one o'clock in the morning
I'm savoring those yet-to-be-cooked tamales
I can't wait
I struggle
my body swollen
nine months pregnant
finally out of the chair and over to the sink
wash my hands
inhale the moment
a sense of regret
walk over to the wood stove to warm my hands
waddle to bed
submit to sleep
with the relish and merit of a laborer
as two hours later

my body is clenched in fists of
birth journey
still I think of tamales even as
my body
shatters the glass case of my mind
yanking
in deep wracking symphony
melancholy sonata
cold dark unforgiving
universe painfully awaiting the bursting sun
my only hope
to make it to the hospital on time
maybe I should have done the birthing class
another contraction
you've seen the movies
just breathe
breathe
breathe
then what
breathe
pray
> *Dios te salve Maria*
> *llena eres de gracia*
> *el Señor es contigo…*

Her only hope is human compassion

In the car
focus on the digital numbers
blinking time
outside temperature
4:14 a.m.
fourteen degrees below zero
thankful for my mom's poncho
a warm blanket
as not even the heated leather seats of the Cadillac
can offer condolence or comfort
as another contraction seizes my body
as all I can do is breathe
pray
>   *Dios te salve Maria*
>   *llena eres de gracia*
>   *el Señor es contigo...*

>   *on a desert road*
>   *astride a beast*
>   *thankful for Her mother's woven blanket*
>   *turned away again*
>   *another contraction seizes Her body*
>   *all She can do is breathe*

I arrive at the hospital
no time to spare

directed to the emergency room
so busy
sounds of suffering tug my heart
static-cling herald angels
on the Admit window
silent
should be a time of peace
another contraction seizes me
I bend over
hold my baby so it will have a warm bed to land
please hurry
don't let me have my baby here
        Dios te salve Maria
        llena eres de gracia
        el Señor es contigo…

                finally someone extends compassion
                a stable with a pile of straw
                animals will provide warmth
                She can go no further
                this will have to do
                She is the handmaid

laid back
spread open
cold operation table

other things to concentrate on
giant convex mirror
reflecting my birth canal
the doctor yelling
push
PUSH
I scoot to the end of the table
squat
push
doctor scolds me onto my back
my body can't withstand
gravitational battle
I scoot to the end of the table
he scolds again
I lie
attempt to push
nothing happens
but body seized in agony again.
 Dios te salve Maria
 llena eres de gracia
 el Señor es contigo...

  laid out on cushion of straw
  scared
  other things to concentrate on
  darkness

stench of animals
faith that all will be well
pain

told my baby's not in position
upside down
not moving
if I can't with the next push
a c-section to save it
he reaches in to re-position the baby
will not budge
must push
no longer stand the pain
about to lose consciousness
thighs quiver in denial
inhale all the life
all the strength
of all the world
filling my lungs
push for a final time
haze between life and death
erased
a blaze of piercing blinding light
     Dios te salve Maria
     llena eres de gracia
     el Señor es contigo…

no longer stand the pain
push for the life of the world
haze between faith and fear
erased
only peace
triumph
blinding light

a girl
presented to me in red furry stocking
kiss each little finger as it clings to mine
lips and cheeks rosy
God's gift to me
my gift to my family
    ... *bendita tu eres entre todas las mujere*
    bendito es el fruto de tu vientre Jesús

    a boy
    presented in strips of His mother's cloth
    She holds His hand in Hers
    stained with blood
    vision of things to come
    God's gift to Her
    Her sacrifice
    to all the world
    for all of time

Santa Maria
madre de Dios
ruega por nosotros pecadores
ahora y en la hora
de nuestro muerte
Amen

now I can go home and eat tamales to my heart's content
te amo, mi'ja
Angelica Noel

Gloria en excelsis Deo.

A SIMPLE RED RIBBON

Mom rinses her own pale face in the bathroom sink
cold water
inability to imagine the task at hand
You've gotta do it mom
you just do
She hands the brush to mom
stands before her at the mirror
It's picture day
all the cheerleaders will have French braids
please mom
you have to
Mom takes the red ribbon from her daughter's hand
separates a trinity of strands at the crown
runs fingers through eleven years of memories
auburn hair gilded in summer
now as November leaves
sparse and crisp from so many months of chemo for lupus
mom avoids the amber reflected
eyes too like her own
tilts the girl's head
begins to weave left in, right in, left
in, right in, left in, right, maybe, left,
right slips, left, right slithers, left falls off
a clump in mom's hand
She tries to hide by dropping into the wastebasket
Yet they both stare at it dead in the trash

I just wanted to be part of a team
says the girl
eyes avoid
Mom rinses her hands
seals her lips white with her teeth
The pink bandana or the white
asks the girl
Pink
Before she even raises eyes from the trash
girl ties on the white
rolls on strawberry lip gloss
smacks
tosses a *sorry, but I look good in white*
over her shoulder as she runs off to school
Mom lingers on the strawberry scent
on the red ribbon in her hand
on the mirror
on the mirror refusing to see her

FALLEN

So you get to keep my love proven as I ooze
yours. Out. You drift off, away, your
back towards me, dream dreams
of who? I hold onto your hips,
pull, scoot closer, fill your
empty space with
roundness of my
own, put my arm
around your belly,
inhale your musk. I
close my eyes, imagine
us as one. Palm cupped to
hollow of your chest, feel your
rise and fall, rise, fall, beats like
jump rope hitting the beaten dirt, rise,
fall, rise and I leap with my own breath,
rise fall, breathe you breathe we breathe
beyond, fluid time, unison, one breath, up
down, in, out… and you stop. I feel, listen,
breathe. You wait 'til mine has left before
you take another. I stroke your skin, so
like the bottom of a chocolate bar, lure
moans stolen from your dream other,
let me in. I match my breathing to
yours again, bob on the lake of us,
fill and float, let me in, yes, so
smooth, aaaahhh, then you
snore and roll over onto
your belly. I roll to
my side, sigh, still
oozing you.

FIRST DANCE

The gym of my old high school beckoned on the hill
much smaller it seemed than when I was there
vaulted windows glinted in the dark
too high to peek in or out
I parked my mom's borrowed station wagon
in the empty teacher's lot facing the door
and wait
radio up to classic rock
console clock blinking the approaching midnight hour
window down to cool apple air
gym doors opened outward for a cluster of boys and two girls
one who whispered with cupped hand
into the other's ear as they stumbled in heels
tugged at the cumbersome bodice of borrowed gowns
followed the boys out
neither girl mine
before the heavy door slammed behind them
a forgotten tune whirled out across the lawn through the
crackle of leaves
tumbling down the hill
Oh no not I
I will… wha??
I remembered that one all too well
a staple of any tape I'd mix off the radio as a kid
turned the radio volume down
flooded with memories
too young for such memories

of a time of wet kisses and bubble gum
loosely rolled joints
Boone's Farm Wine—Wild Island or Strawberry Hill
swapped amidst dust bunnies
crushed soda cans
hidden in cavern of wood metal bleachers and
wallflower bottoms peeking through
rhythm pumping
strobe light thumping
working a sweat
remember again

how quickly fifteen years had gone by
her first high school dance
reminded me how much time had passed
how much she had overcome from the moment she was born
and grown into her name
I had no idea would be the most popular girl's name of 1988
although for nine months I hashed it over in my mind
I had not come up with a good name for her
whole pregnancy caught me off guard

I had just moved in with her dad
his roommate had kicked him out
for hooking up with me
when he thought he had first dibs

as brother to my best friend's boyfriend
who had kicked me out
of my best friend's house
for refusing his secret proposals

I had enough
learning to be homemaker
roommate
partner
lover
grown up
woman
unaware of what to do
think
say
about being a mother
I needed a moment
before I could admit to my parents
their suspicion was correct
no longer able to dance around the truth
my lie was just that
not living with my best friend
as was my intent
but living with the man ten years older than me
who had taken me in

we took a road trip
to figure things out
a visit with his people in San Antonio
you'll love it there
if so
we'll come back
pack it all up
start somewhere new
my roads all led west
don't take much to lure me with someplace new
at the time awaiting unemployment approval
from a night club deejay job
would no longer miss me
with a baby bump
part of my attraction was
my ability to shake my ass all night
in between songs and dance mixes
keep that dance floor filled
the booths empty
clients hot sweaty and thirsty
a job I was born for
prepared for all my life
mixing tapes off the radio
accustoming myself to the unfamiliar sound
     of my announcer voice
auditioned for a week to win that position

all the competition experienced men with their own equipment
I was nineteen
not even old enough to legally drink
but I'd been drinking since I was ten
and much the pro right around then
got the job
was a great job
until I understood the play
between my boss and the bartender
brothers
in the family that owned and ran the bar
owned to give them a proper stage
where my boss was the star and twice my age
played his own saxophone sets every night
recognized the wannabe Tom Jones desire for panties
        thrown on his stage
he'd choose a young girl client each night
give the signal to his younger brother behind the bar
mixing drinks his only talent in a show biz family
mixing them real good
to be served to the chosen girl
one night that girl was me
eve of Valentine's Day
needed no help in attracting free drink
each night I could collect one for each dedicated song
the nights were long

and I danced enough to drink them all
until that night
drink after drink was poured for me
special mix from the bar I was told
a new drink for me to critique
named after the brother with no song
Val
Valyum
waitress who had been girl of the night some time
    the last week
must've brought three
so I was prepared for the worst when he
boxed me in the darkest corner behind
    the deejay booth
pinned
skirt grabbed and uplifted
lips suckling for my neck
that crushing alcohol breath
he refused my NO
I was able to fight him off
only went back at the end of the week for my check
mom, dad, brothers
all worked there
all knew why
so they would fight it and
I was denied unemployment

insufficient funds to return
our weekend trip to Texas to figure things out lasted
        half a year

I told my parents about my pregnancy six months in
called from a payphone
in the laundry room of our apartment complex
because I could not take the lie anymore
far enough to escape their disappointment
tinge of relief in knowing I was at least alive
think I heard my dad cry
for the first time

I did not like San Antonio
so hot and humid
spent my time there as a puddle
thought we'd try our luck in Los Angeles
my birth place
first home
headed back there at last
was just like I remembered
but nothing like I could expect
took months to be approved for Medicaid
made a prenatal appointment for the very first day
        I'd be covered
February first

with the only doctor I could find that still accepted
    Medicaid
my water broke January thirty-first
no Medicaid card yet shown up in the mail
all I had was the card number
scrawled by my caseworker on scrap paper
when I showed up to my 4:45 doctor's appointment
bent at the waist
in full-on labor
trying to keep baby tucked in
'til I made it to the door
receptionist on the phone for minutes
before she took notice of me
at that moment I couldn't breathe
wracked by another labor pain
had to grab on to the countertop to remain upright
explained the situation once I could breathe again
receptionist laughed
girl, you are not having that baby here
without no insurance card
don't care what your paper says
you best hope you get your caseworker on this phone
to tell me you're approved
or else
you ain't having that baby here
but I was already having that baby

goddess was with me that day
caseworker answered her phone
a minute before five
anyone on public assistance will tell
what a miracle that is
before I had a chance to grunt out my labor
old man doctor I'd never seen before
for no reason but patriarchal ones
slit me open with a blade
straight razor shaved my pubic hair
screamed at that pain I was totally unprepared for
unnecessary blood
husband stitch

three pushes and she was out
placed on my belly
at the moment the doctor gasped
oh no
I saw her face in profile
of a cleft palate
a bit of profusion and gap
between the nose and the lip
something I had no prior conception of
she was crying so strong
I had no idea what was wrong
she was taken from me in that moment

crying
kept in the nurse's station all night long
I could hear her cry
so loud
a cry I knew above all the others coming from the nursery
I knew her cry
her song
my family members standing around speechless
wanting so much to celebrate
with their banners and balloons
just waiting
waiting to find out what was wrong
the whispers unreal to bear
my guess is they had all seen her before me
based on expressions as they walked in the room
discussions already had
including Fedelina
my grandma
declaring I had stained the Martinez bloodline
something I didn't know until after her death

stuck in the limbo of my daughter's abandoned cry
wondering if she would live or die
I will survive
until someone had the courage to come tell me
     what was going on

a nurse who worked the graveyard shift
who herself had been born with it
a defect
yes
mostly cosmetic in its effect

well then
what is the problem
bring her to me
I said

they did not
until she needed to be dressed the next morning
for transfer to the neonatal ICU at Long Beach
        Children's Hospital
they reluctantly placed her in my arms and left me alone

she was the most beautiful thing I'd ever seen
angel's face to contrast the night's
bloodcurdling motherless screams
she calmed so quickly
I picked her up close to inspect the form of her mouth
inside and out
seemed like all the parts were there
a few puzzle pieces
shaken a bit loose from their connective grooves

nothing shameful as their separation of the two of us
in that first moment when we most needed one another

and it suddenly came to me
Amanda
was the perfect name
for one would be so loved
it would be ten long days sitting with her in ICU
making sure she could intake enough milk
through the medicine dropper they gave
until the cleft palate bottles came
enough milk to survive
I will
before they let me bring her home

she did not like the darkness
stayed awake all damned night
cried and cried
no rocking or singing could keep her quiet
unless it was a slow dance hummed with
her nestled in my chest
my otherwise useless leaking breasts
and we'd dance all night
until her dad left to work.
Was four months
before she slept through the night

and only right at my side
where I could hear her heartbeat and she mine
four months
until the surgery to close the gap in her lip
like she knew
her draft was finally complete

and there we were
she no longer considered herself just a girl
she was ready to escape into the world
after a childhood of bringing home strays and the
gym door opened and slammed shut again
bringing me back
I checked the time on my radio clock
really
only five minutes have passed
damn
I should have said eleven
what was I thinking midnight
for her first high school dance?
I'd try not to sniff her as she sat next to me
like my mom did to me anytime I'd been out
and then came another
familiar song in the night
tried to focus on the music that time
not the memories

I shook my head
lit a roach I had brought in the ashtray
to soften the wait
stepped onto blacktop in pink bunny slippers
leaned on the fender
turned my pockets inside-out
in search of twenty years

they say we remain stuck in the place and time
we were loved the least

I listened for the next song
fought the urge to become my mother
worried about how the more things change
ah, shut the fuck up
and wait
I said to my own hopeless mind
my brown-eyed girl
at her watch a glance
time for one last dance
maybe two

ODE to JENNIFER

Hey mom,
can Jennifer come over to play?
Her mom took off with her boyfriend to L.A.
Who knows when she'll be back, she won't even say.

And this is the mom you told me was cool?
If you ask me she's a penis-whipped fool
      not giving a damn if her daughter's in school.

I know, but mom,
Jen's cutting again.
You know she's been doing it since we were ten and
she says I'm her only, one and true friend.
So mom,
can she come over to stay?
She told me she hasn't eaten all day
her mom's sending money but there's rent to pay.

I can't believe she left her alone
her only defense a pinche cell phone
how could she think that at fourteen she's grown?
Didn't she learn her lesson back then?
I mean, her daughter raped by the time she was ten
by her own on-again, off-again junkie boyfriend.

I don't know, mom,
but I'm worried for her
alone in that building I know I'd be scared.
I've seen drunk old men come in and out of there
leaving bottles and needles thrown in the halls
the smell of piss on the carpet and walls
so mom, pleeeease
can she come over to stay?
I promise it'll be just for one day…

CIGARETTE CHANGE

drove by your house today
saddened as I remembered how clean you kept your yard
sad to see how tall the weeds had grown
littered
bags spilling trash
remnants of taco bell you probably scraped your last change for
a break from cooking again
cleaning after one more meal
your last there
which you would have simmered in the crock pot had you known
now ghosts of paper whirl across the dirt
swirling pirouettes then pinned against the fence
you were a mother then
stiffened jeans on the line
joking in the air,
mop-n-glo shine
incense of that last tortilla that always burns
that always gets eaten by you
you with a double bed to greet you cold
with that mother-in-law's plant wandering through your kitchen
        and living room
strung to the ceiling with kite string and yellow push pins
alive and wild and breathing
always wondered how you'd ever move that thing without harm
and your daughter chasing your son threatening to break his arm
if he read her diary again

a family then
with bags of garbage tied neatly
waiting on the curb
don't know who called the cops
did you really think the white lines
little glass pipe
gorra
spurious scrips for pinks, yellows and blues
would dull them
the blues
and warm your feet at night
because now you're gone and but a phone call
     on weekends to
those kids for whom you'd scrape your last
     cigarette change to buy taco bell
and the smells of the bags never picked up
vex the neighborhood dogs.

PAST MY PEAK in the GYNO'S OFFICE

early for a one o'clock appointment
squirming in my seat in the lobby
doctor doesn't call me back 'til two
my bladder now wants revenge
in explosion spray as he tinkers inside
questioning me from between my own knees
are you
sexually active?
wha?
he knows my age
why I'm here
I'd like to see him ask that of a teenaged boy
all gray and love handles aside
do I really look past my peak?
first day of my last cycle?
six weeks... hell I don't...
Ratched walks me down the hall
first door to the right
finally
thank god
yeah, yeah
antiseptic wipe
front to back
fill at midstream
of course I will wash my hands afterward geez
aaaaaaahhhhhh

oh shit overfill
overspill
damn!
wipe up
wash up
leave deposit in the drawer
walk back to which room?
what a maze
room number two
sit
wait
check time

2:09. feet tap to tune of favorite corrído—wait
no—no favorite
women in dance halls
women at bars
women at home minding their affairs
killed by jealous husband or boyfriend
Maldad Y Traiciones
feet tap anyhow
chew nails
pace two pace-able square yards
what was I thinking?
I know better than to mount the saddle
sperm swim straight up

needed to be touched
felt
felt up
needed his milk-chocolate flesh
against my flabby thirsty relenting begging sighing clenching
don't scream
screaming self
ugh

2:14. why do doctors' mirrors always exaggerate?
backside's worse than the front
fat ass that ain't really ass
only mushrooming hips
if I am pregnant
I'll eat and eat and eat
they'll have to tear out door jambs to get me out
forklift me into the delivery room
my sister all up in my thing
snatching video of my stretched-out stirruped glory
hole oozing bodily fluids
what was I thinking!
no birthing room videos please!
aah where in the hell is that pínche nurse?

2:19. any day now
plus or minus

positive or negative
half empty
half full
a boy
I'd name Luciano
they'd call him Lucky
he'd be… feb… may… aug… november?
scorpio
great thinkers
no, don't think
just time to cut out the goodies
maybe just fats in general
carbs, yeah, carbs
but not all of them
what good would life be
without the love of a warm buttery tortilla
squashed into a chewy ball?
especially if
with all the no drinking, no smoking and shit?

2:24. oh my
will he think it's his?
he'll want to name him
after himself
whose hair would he have?
eyes?

could be a girl
no girls
enough girls
girls hate and leave
boys love and stay
how long
twenty years
thought I was done
I'll be… ahshit,
too gray anyhow
alone
better off
lonely
well hell
there's always Manuelito and his five friends, haha
he'd need all ten thank you very much
while we're on the subject—

ohgodthenurse

SPARE KEY

A dollar thirty-three
it costs to be free
a mere one thirty-three
if you had known your keys would be thrown
in deep, dark pocket of his heart
irretrievable
inconceivable
that he would give a head-start
the price of a key
one thirty-three
would set you free
instead you sit as he pitches his fit
beg your mouth to keep shut
no longer feeling attempts at concealing
echoes of walk bitch slut
don't say a word
just watch the little bird flitter innocently by
you'll never win by jumping right in
so please don't even try
it'll be over soon
you know the tune
word for word is stomped on your heart
funny how he doesn't hear the damage in fear
the echoes of falling apart
don't even think of trying to run
he'll catch you and all will be worse
just remember
a mere one thirty-three
will buy a spare key for your purse.

BROKEN WINDOW

sun shattered
spilled to loam
a honeycomb of mirrors
a million eyes tinkle
collected
tumble the years inside the lint trap of your pocket
glisten as shards you carry home
to paste upon your crayon collage

daily you return for my jagged gaping holding-on
but the more you retrieve
the more you are bit
by bit-by-bit license to whistle the wind
gulping
sweet as your flesh caught and reflection denied

dawn scattered is essence released
pieces you pocket to keep me in
are pieces that actually set me free
sunlight never forgets
I am open to all
and all open to me and
it is you who bleeds to fill my pane.

MILESTONES

Forty years old
I reached a milestone that day
a hundred thousand milestone
but I was fine; good with it.
The day was gilded;
the evening moon dance cool—
your numbers, your odds bet he would find his way
into the county jail. You won.
BCJDC to be exact.
Mexican clique
he says, Juaritos, East side
been hassling me since summer mom you know that,
talking trash because I don't understand.

Twelve years and seems
my son reached a milestone too.
One you all knew he would being brown and all.
Aggravated assault with a deadly weapon, your report states.
Knife opened, blade snarling.
Who wants to die first
you say he said.
Told you I'd end up in trouble at that school.
They surrounded me,
thirty of them cussin' at me in Spanish.
I threw my notebook down, pulled out the knife, unopened
held it in my closed hand
told them hit me, c'mon, who's gonna hit me first.

Wasn't gonna let them beat the crap out of me.
Same gang that shot at Pep's house, remember?
Shot his brother and cousin—we saw it on the news.
I'm sorry mom, he cried.
It sucks in here.

His dad and I drive over to BCJDC.
We need him home. Tears roll
all the way. He's been there all day.
I'm sorry, my boy.
I'm the reason you look brown but speak beige.
Brown, and then not brown enough.
Nothing we can do when it's
a charge like this, so many points
says the white female officer
at the bulletproof window, repeating the charge.

How old? Twelve.
Is he in a gang? No.
Do drugs? No.
Grade?
Seventh.
Grades?
A's, B's.
Just made the basketball team
Practices every day.
Gonna be Randy Moss someday,

on the cover of *Sports Illustrated*
after taking the Broncos to the Super Bowl.
Loves to cook.
Read.
Stand up for his friends.
Speak up for himself.
Defy.

You're young
she says to him
let's see what I can do.
Gonna ask you some pretty personal questions right now
gonna ask your mom to step out of the room.
Why?
My mom's gonna be a lawyer
my lawyer
and she's my mom
and she needs to know
so she stays.
Ask away.
She did.
I saved my tears related to the answers for another time
wondered where the fuck was I
where had I been
that I'd not seen.
She makes a couple of phone calls,
receives another.

Seems her son reached a milestone too.
You did?!?
Oh, I'm so proud of you!
You did potty in the potty chair!
Mommy is so proud of you, my big boy!
Gotta go, can't talk right now,
but gimme a high five!
That's my boy!

Wonder if he'd ever
still pee the bed at night
while his dad yelled at his mom
or if he'd ever be handcuffed
in front of his friends
teachers watching in disbelief
principal
browner than he,
who sang "Happy Birthday" to him
over the intercom on his second day at the new school?
Would her boy see the inside of BCJDC,
or only from mom's front desk?
We sign some papers.
He'll be on twenty-four-hour house arrest. No friends,
    no acquaintances.
No school. No football. 'Til he sees the judge.

We take him home… for now.

LITMUS

it is told that Grandma Lou's hair turned gray overnight
when she got the news that the boys died
my mom's brothers
three of them
died together
carbon monoxide poisoning
gas leak in their apartment
nineteen, twenty, twenty-two years old
one a brand-new dad
grandma was forty-four when her hair turned white
overnight
was the myth
what I believed to be
myth
thing about myth
each begins with some truth
some begin at facing some truth

mine came in the ER
the year I turned forty
as I stared at the curtain pulled around my hospital bed
dumbstruck
pulmonary embolism was the diagnosis
blood clot in the lung
I should have died
I know the moment
felt as if I'd had a stake pounded straight through my heart

I sprang up in bed
couldn't catch my breath
couldn't feel my chest
couldn't feel myself
all I could do was gape in terror
in silence
my body frozen as my lights went dim
I felt myself falling forward off the bed
then I felt a yank backwards
pounding between my shoulder blades
pounding
pounding hard
until I felt as if a cork popped inside my heart
and I gasped back into the light
Eli had saved my life
not only by dislodging the clot which had stopped
        my heart
but earlier he had convinced me to
come upstairs to bed
I'd been sleeping on the couch for a week
forced to sleep sitting up from the pain
had just started a new job
no sick leave
Eli would have never heard a thing
I would have died on the couch
for my kids to find
and it was my fault

I had been at the emergency room the day before
for the same thing
so happy when I saw the doctor that called me back
looked like me
woman
about the same age
last name same as mine
felt I was in good hands
I was not there long
told I had "viral syndrome"
whatever the fuck
sounds like you are saying it's all in my head
I said
she chuckled
yeah, something like that
it could be anything

but I'm coughing up clumps of blood
I reminded her
but she sent me home anyway

I was mad at myself for having missed a midterm exam for that
went back to campus
back to class
had to leave class because of the pain
that never stopped
dragged my ass across the campus

because I had no cell phone
tried to walk home but
fell to a crawl and had to call home from an emergency
     campus phone

went to the ER
waited hours before I was called back
given a shot of heaven
I mean morphine
immediately
I fell asleep
thankful for a break from the pain
woke to the sound of a doctor yelling at the nurses
     in the nurses' station
asking *who was the doctor that saw her last night*
that just sent her home to die
somebody here knows
I want to know now
get me her chart
and get her bed rolled out here close by
you are all in charge of her now
every one of you
wondered about that poor soul
in my dazed state
why that doctor was so mad
when came a knock on my door

orderly rolled me out
parked my bed right next to the nurse's station
that was the moment I knew I should've been dead
but I still did not know why

doctor showed up shortly afterward
clipboard in hand
pulmonary embolism
worked its way through my heart to my lung
lucky
he said
I'd chosen to sleep in my bed
otherwise
the moment I felt
would've been my moment of death

do you smoke?
asked the doctor
not cigarettes
was my answer
he nodded in understanding
birth control?
yes
regularly?
nope

he disappeared around the curtain again
said I'd be getting an MRI and x-ray
to find where the clot came from
to see if there were more

my focus settled on the ugly southwest-style curtain
enclosing me
made me nauseated to look at
loomed in human tissue colors
as if seeped in litmus stripes from the emergency room floor
tongue pink
matter gray
liver red
blood blue
jaundice yellow
bile green
alternating shades of each color
stacked like building blocks
the more I looked
the more they took the form of some cryptic bar graph of
possibly every joint I had smoked in my life
I counted
I tend to count things
one hundred sixty stripes across
sixty blocks per stripe
I multiplied

dropped the zeroes
carried the three...
ninety-six hundred
divided by twenty years
about one and a half joints a day
which was my god probably about right
staggering to see for someone who considered herself
    a non-smoker
I closed my eyes and let Darvocet have its way

I was admitted and moved to a second-floor room
after eighteen hours in the ER
confirmed it was a pulmonary embolism
confirmed they found no other clots
confirmed likely caused by the hormones in
    birth control pills
I knew my body did not like birth control
but I was guilted into taking it
after I birthed each of my kids
usually only did it for a few months
but being in college full time since JuanAndrés was born
I stayed on the pill
I was so busy I would forget to take them some days
take two the next
stupid shit
was all I could think

careless
the only person I ever knew that had a blood clot
died a week after her diagnosis
she was fifteen
doctor came back
said a few things I didn't hear
said I would be on blood thinners
said I would have to inject myself
twice a day for a month
in the soft of my belly

so no more smoking that funny weed, right?
doctor said
especially because you're over thirty-five and
a bit hefty
felt like garbage

and if you're a drinker
we need to know
because alcohol works as a blood thinner
and we'd have to keep adjusting your dosage
so avoid it as much as possible and
try to lose some weight
and remember
no pill
no patch

no hormones
ever
wow
I thought
let me get this shit straight
no smoking
no eating
no drinking
no fucking

just put me out to pasture then
I thought
because if I get there anyway
menopause will be the death of me
or everyone around me
was all I could think

it was around five o'clock
about time for my siblings to arrive
I grabbed my makeup bag
locked myself in the bathroom to gather my thoughts
swallow my tears
put on my face

I had not seen my reflection in hours
when my attention finally settled on the mirror

I saw my hair
had turned white
overnight
my entire crown
white
I dropped my makeup bag in disbelief
shattered my compact mirror
no longer felt the need to apply lipstick
crawled back under the sickly smelling sheet
tried my best to fall asleep
before anyone had a chance to wander in.

LATE NIGHT 66

Saunter by the window of a well-lit joint after a longlong day
see feta crumbles on crisp spinach salad
carafe of red wine
they dine at a table for two with a checkerboard cloth
holding eyes across settings
as you dart your own
because you've just a dollar for bus fare

Stop
wait beside the spilling trash
outside a new window
a bar that fixes shrimp platters for warm democrats
who stir and sip margaritas
crunch on ice and savor coarse salt from the rim

You turn and hell no
dude must think you've a bag of tricks
way he licks his lips
whistles each time he circles the block in his cancered
      pick-up truck
so you walk slowly on past and over the shoes of
lives being sucked inside glass bottles
disguised as brown paper bags
like the tricks being turned by a twig of a girl
maybe eighteen
stumbles onto Central from an unlit alley

pants undone
eyes glazed
sunken mouth
bare feet
offering fun to everyone she meets
taken by the driver of a blue minivan
through a sliding back door
baby seat in the back
erase that if you can

Outrun the bus to the next stop
get on at last
hope that stinky ass don't sit by you
in greasy Levi's he's slept and sweated
smoked stroked petted and scratched his balls
        all-week-long in
glad to see instead you get a skinny dude
in a self-proclaimed righteous mood
tells a friend that his twenty-first birthday is Friday and
all he really needs to set himself free are
two fat chicks and a fat green stash and
you try not to laugh and
take home hope for the world from wherever you can
'cause damn
tonight it's ramen for dinner again

WOMEN of BURQUE

Those eyes, you've seen them
smolder of blue-black
kind that don't look back
the still-poor
poor
the still-young dying before they're spent
wondering what they meant
when they said repent
not really concerned with boundaries

west mesa bone collector
made a left turn at Burque
of half a million
where women can vanish into thin air
without anyone giving a shit
buried in the basalt blue-black west mesa borderlands
ancestral petroglyphs
trash dumps, spent slugs, blasted-out targets
hundred-acre boneyard scene
"crime of the century"

Cinnamon
Doreen
Evelyn
Jamie

Julie
Michelle
Monica
Syllania
Veronica
Victoria
Virginia
baby unborn

broken discarded bones
of the less alive
now the less dead
nothing
but a list of missing hookers
to cops who made no effort to find them
APD declines to comment
everyone's a theory and yet
no incentive to investigate
what victims had coming
a man's gotta be tougher than the timber he's cutting
perhaps as Cinnamon told friends
before her untimely end
that "a dirty cop
was chopping off the heads of prostitutes and
burying them on the west mesa"

now I'm no stranger to the street
but just eleven days
after DOJ condemned APD for brutality
APD's Jeremy Dear
shot and killed
nineteen-year-old Mary Hawkes
pretty,
petite,
maybe eighty-nine pounds wet
hawk eyes
younger than her street wise
loved horses
but homeless
daughter of a sitting judge
known to sleep in unlocked cars
with a knack for evading APD
trying to catch her in that act
until her last
because blue lies matter

Dear was literally at Dunkin' Donuts
when the call came
surely a hard-on when he heard her name
didn't catch her in the act
but knew he had to act fast

"facing me, I stared down the barrel of her gun"
 yet the bullets that killed her came from the side
         and above

"so close I could see the silver on the tip where the black
         gun was scratched"
 yet no blood spatter
 no DNA
 no fingerprint or evidence to match

"I was scared to death
 never been more scared in my life
 I didn't want to die"
 all a lie
 as in truth
 he'd pumped three bullets
 not into her spritely frame
 but aimed at her head from above
 bullets say
 she was on her knees
 or falling
 as they blazed white
 down through her head
 throat
 clavicle

oozing out her armpit
Dear again
with no camera plugged in
not since the last time it caught him
in another white lie
about another gun in the hands of
another dead unarmed man
and the other cop's cam video
city-sanctioned tampered
because blue lies matter

the only remorse Dear ever media-quipped was
having had to walk the beat "because of that fucking bitch"

day after day the city paid a crew
to have her name erased
sidewalk chalk tags
teddy bears
handwritten notes
candles aglow in Virgen of the Rainbow
left at the murder scene
by a community enraged
in pain
erased
day after day

after goddamned day
the still-poor
poor
the still-young dying before their time

nothing but black-and-blue lives

but black-and-blue lives
are black matter
sure as love is first born of chaos.

THE GAME of LIFE aka 1L CON RIGHTS RACE CASE POETRY for DUMMIES

life is law
so we've read
race deliberated in context from the poll to the bed
does it indicate status, community, physical traits
or the subordinate badge of historical race?
perhaps it's the Constitutional wording that troubles us so
as the framers are gone how the hell do we know?
do we look at each word and assume what it meant
or at the use of those words to establish intent?
does the law construct our understanding of race
or is law a reflection of our own social face?
let's analyze life and equal protection
cast a roll of the dice
assume a direction

want to marry, have kids, and start a new life?
like white construction worker Richard Loving
took his black high school sweetheart Mildred Jeter for his wife
married in D.C. where their union was legal and certified
proof hanging on the bedroom wall of their Virginia home
but in _Loving v. Virginia_, the state invaded their bed
sheriffs posted outside their bedroom windows at night
had to catch them fucking
or just giving head
to warrant the arrest
one year suspended sentence

in exchange for twenty-five-year exile outside
  Virginia state lines
we have legitimate purpose Virginia decreed
to prevent procreation of a new mongrel breed!
but this time the Court disagreed finding
marriage is a basic civil right of all *men*
or so Justice Warren decreed

now you are married and happy but don't get settled in
there's a war to be fought, one we must win
In 1942 if you're Japanese-American, you've got to go
turn yourself in
take your family and check in
internment camps built throughout the desert southwest
twenty-three-year-old Fred Korematsu refused
stood his ground
said *no I won't go*
had plastic surgery on his eyes
changed his name to Clyde Sarah to reflect
  his American side
arrested for failure to report
to a relocation center aka concentration camp
Korematsu v. U.S. ruled detention a "military necessity"
  regardless of race
in 1983 ACLU re-opened his case
based on FBI intelligence suppressed or destroyed

conviction overturned
in the same courthouse
he'd been convicted forty-one years before

now if you have kids you'll need to send them to school
Brown v. Board has established the rule
that separate is not equal protection of rights
but this cost Southern senators much sleep in their nights
when the Court ruled desegregate at "all deliberate speed"
so resistance by states found ways to supersede
cut funding
close schools
mandate segregation
the children of _Brown_ never reaped what they sowed
but kids of _Milliken v. Bradley_ taken by busload
far away from their homes
many districts away
as again in in the name of furthering rights
seems it is always black children that pay then

all grown up
going off to college
perhaps historical race will aid in their quest for knowledge
but don't let your sons of color
college in a white town
racial profiling

may have cops hunting them down
on a claim of attempted burglary
by an aged white woman
rounded up and detained in *Brown v. City of Oneonta*
along with every other brother of color in town
for being Brown

maybe the luck of the dice leads you down the wrong road
where a prison cell awaits as your new abode and
an immutable trait such as skin color
overwhelmingly decides
in *McClesky v. Kemp* whether you live or you die
maybe the court can't decide if you're black or you're white
 if you're somewhere between
in *Hernandez v. Texas* you may lose your right
to a trial by jury
bilingual like you
where translation of testimony
is fractured and untrue
you see, the game of life and law
is always being played
roll again
now
with gender decisions to be made.

Loving v. Virginia, 338 U.S. 1 (1967).
Korematsu v. United States, 323 U.S. 214 (1944).
Brown v. Board of Education of Topeka, Kansas, 347 U.S.
    483 (1954).
Milliken v. Bradley, 418 U.S. 717 (1974).
Brown v. City of Oneonta, 221 F3d 329 (2d Cir. 1999).
McClesky v. Kemp, 481 U.S. 279 (1987).
Hernandez v. Texas, 347 U.S. 475 (1954).

REMATCH

You look at me like you could crack that stick over my skull. Instead you whack the thick end on the unrelenting wood floor.

Good game, your lips mutter, how about best three out of five? You're on, I say, figuring I owe you for that date that didn't work out.

You fold at the waist, lower your chest to the table, draw eyebrows together. Eyes reflect the green as you fill, grip, shake the rack and lift, pick and grind

your stick in a cube of blue, focus on the spot that will rocket colored balls from pocket to pocket, lay tip of cue on the skin hammock that sways between trigger finger and thumb, stop, take a scripted sip from a can of warm beer, set, and wipe a hand over your wallet pocket.

I flash my ivory, lick my lips as you re-grip your stick, fold at the waist, lower your chest to the table

and break.

KILLING STUMP

The one who has the bride is the bridegroom.
The friend of the bridegroom, who stands and hears him,
rejoices greatly at the bridegroom's voice.
Therefore this joy of mine is now complete.
He must increase, but I must decrease.
                    John 3:29-30

They say there is a moment during the labor of childbirth
where the mother straddles worlds
ten-centimeter crown
to birth one new
dark side of the emergence of the head
one foot on either side
life and death
as the child's shoulders rip through her exit
her opening
stretched to torn
the last hold onto the warmth of the womb
from choking gasp watery death
to the first gush of living breath
that takes every last of hers to provide
like a levee break
for me that moment came
explosion in my brain
tumbled in foaming wave of
profuse white light
WOWWWwwwhoa

that's the one
said a whisper in my head
warning me not to be swept in the pull

"He looks like a Juan"
surely yanked me back as
what the hell
said the whisper next
we had not told anyone we planned on
naming him JuanAndrés
after both grandpas
two men so dedicated to honor the mother
each found goddess in his own way
in his own god
one tapped into nature
the other tapped into his soul
both tapped into divinity
JuanAndrés
I had not even seen my son's face yet
nor the doctor that had said it as
he had slipped into place between my stirruped legs
while I was in that space
literally walked in just in time to catch him
and breathe my son's yet-unspoken name.
Juan
John

born on the birthday of the Virgen
September 8

also the anniversary of the
dedication of the very first church in San Juan
in what would be the very first European capital
        of our homeland
that would eventually be called the
new Mexico

So we began at a crossroads
pueblos
across rivers
river crossroads
Yunque
on the north side
Ohkay Owingeh
on the south
on the spot where the motherland
was first thrust by the white man's flag
first Spanish capital in the alleged New World
San Juan Bautista
St. John the Baptist
between rivers
worlds
pueblos

centuries
nations
God and mother
Yunque abandoned its township for the invader
        to move right in
without having to build

The Yunque joined the Ohkay Owingeh in the south
to make room for the white god the white men
        had brought
so history said

on that crossroads
they built a church named for the Baptist
nature tore it down
they built a bigger church
then a French priest rebuilt that church French
and added a stone chapel that mirrored it to honor
        the Lady of Fatima
in the New Mexico
and my grandmother
Lucia's mom was
charged with keeping her chapel flowered and clean
when her older sister died by suicide
when her husband named Juan left her for a woman
        in Mexico
who got him killed

decapitated
his body sent back
now a tombstone in the churchyard

The cosmic shift began when we named our son
JuanAndrés Jesús
named for our fathers
though regardless of its writing he'd never be called
        by his full name
Juan to the world
Andrés for himself when he could
Aqua to his friends
he likes that

but his dad's mother Rose did not like him
for representing what she saw as the sins of the father
as my son's father
her son
had invented an affair which allegedly led
        to my pregnancy
affairs
in truth his own
with countless women is now my guess
but back then
in a fateful lie to his mother,
mine
his excuse to escape from me

to escape claiming a fourth child
with me
a woman that would never meet the godly standards
required by his mother
whom he loved and once protected
from a father once drunk with guilt now sober
   and penitent
protected for her weak heart
a paternal lie he told
which gave her sweet relief
a revenge she could act upon
in retaliation
for the one-night stand Juan had had
so many years back
resulting in pregnancy
and his sin
a girl
looked more like Juan than his daughter with Rose
who allowed the girl to be part of their lives
but the girl was always herself dying inside
so many suicide attempts
slit her own throat open
one time
trying to find a place in a family
that reminded her day after day that she was a mistake

they say the Christ began when the prophet lost his head
sheared off like a rabbit's
on order of the king
served upon a platter to a dancing girl
daughter of the queen
who demanded the prophet's life
for denouncing their adulterous ways
a double-edged sword
dance to stave off his lust in exchange
for the prophet's head on a plate
for calling out their sin
woe unto them
wise in their own eyes
John sent to bear witness about the light
but he was not the light
and a prophet is not without honor
except in his hometown
and among his relatives

Johnny and Rose had a big family wedding
married at the church of San Juan
then ten years later
so did my parents
Andrés and Lucia and
so

I too tried to marry my children's father there
asked him four times
at the first bloodless sign of
each of my pregnancies with him
but he never agreed to marry me there
or anywhere
it's just a slip of paper
government's way of keeping tabs
he'd say even though he'd been married before
to legitimize the birth of his first daughter
though that marriage lasted but a couple of years and
I myself remain to this day unmarried
now with no expectations of it
ever
though I've lived a life avoiding regret
there is one
how I denied my father that chance
that ceremony
to walk me down the aisle of his church
to know
I'd be loved
eternally
unconditionally
not like he loves me but
like he loves his Lucia

but I've not known that
which is my shame
rivers of tears
nobody likes to hear you cry

Our moms were both from San Juan Bautista
each from either side of the river
both within earshot of the church bell at San Juan
his mom from the north side
Yunque
only girl in a family of sons
protected for her sickly heart
rheumatic from a childhood bout of scarlet fever
scarred
impervious to hugs
tightening
dying
with every breath
every beat
in her house a place for everything
(but hugs)
(tears)
everything in its place
she paid a woman biweekly to keep it that way
fifty dollars a day

for the two-day job
of cleaning her beautiful house
(that she rarely left
except for routine excursions into town)
for cleanliness is next to godliness
no one's home was immaculate as hers and
she was protective of her accumulated things
taught her kids to value the same
her house a temple
built by her husband Juan
Johnny to her
named Juan as he was born on the feast day of the Baptist
June 24
the only saint whose birthday
is celebrated by the church
besides the Virgen and her son of course
all the other saint feast days are
death days

June 24
Día de San Juan
midsummer's day
which once had been dedicated to the fertile abundance
    of a mother god
at one time represented by the hare
now represented by a martyr
stolen into the sky

robbed of humanity
not even allowed human death
ritual mourning
no cuerpo presente
burial
no human song
rebirth
a vision of sin to the god that moved in
sin washed away in desert waters by he named
        for the herald of the king
a voice in the desert
this is my son, of whom I am well pleased
June 24
the day the pueblo waters are blessed
no swimming allowed in her waters until then
the day the rains come
and as local legend has it
any Juan born on this day
had the power to cast magic in the form of prayer
Johnny had called upon that magic before
it was heard
on some guy had stabbed him in a bar fight
a mechanic crushed to death underneath his own car
hapless accident

Johnny was a rancher from birth
animal husbandry his church

had the fattest cows around and
kept a menagerie for his kids
horses as pets and he
had a green thumb like no one else
kept those temple grounds
manicured lawns
roses and fruit trees
fountains and feeders
buzzing with bees and butterflies
constant thrum of hummingbird wings
caw of peacocks strutting finery
cage of bunnies of all bunny hues
named by the kids on whose dinner plates
those bunnies would find their end
beheaded
atop the stump of a once-mighty tree

arboreal mate to the one that had lived
cut down for the aesthetic of
lawn and rose
lighthouse of a cottonwood
beacon of agricultural river valleys
guardian of the acequia
over a century or two
life blood of generations
now cornerstone shelter of manic cured yard
its mate

the one that had lived
forever marked in embittered bark
with the stain of the beheaded bunnies' blood
spattered from the killing stump
like the testimonial cloth
blood image in the shape of the penitent virgin and
her gateway of sin
dismembered
to have her remembered as
dismembered

Juan honored her by tending to her fragile creations
from before the sun rose until after it set

Blood offerings his son could not handle so
inability to become the father
was the true sin of the son
I always wondered what flashed across his mind
as he helped his dad and held each bunny down
soft
steadied from their desperate wiggling
wrists scratched from pointless attempts at escape
cries of anguish from seeing the ones ahead of them go first
readied to be bashed in the head to unconsciousness
in compassionate mercy
before their beheading
creatures raised with daily prayer

love
cuddles
fed the sweetest alfalfa and the choice veggie scraps
sacrificed in offering to her pot
the kids just could not get enough of her rabbit and rice
insatiable contrition for one night of passion that
resulted in immediate conception
daily decapitation
daily bread in offering to her pot
where nothing was really cooked as much as
placed on the lowest gas stove flame and
all day slow simmered to gray

Rose had a quadruple bypass surgery late in her days
to channel her heart open enough to beat
and in the beat of her final breaths
she had a message for me
before I had a chance to cry
unknown my eyes would remain dry
she took the breath to remind me I still owed her
        two thousand dollars
that I should have the decency to pay before she died
which I did not
could not
pay
her funeral held at the church of San Juan
to which I was not invited

followed months later
by the funeral of her Johnny
at which I sat at his son's side
by request
of course everyone expected
the son
to take over the ranch when the burial was done
not knowing
the son could handle the work
but not the blood

and the animals sold for slaughter
and the yard overgrown
and the house dusty and empty

and the son
now seeks approval
by giving things
inanimate objects he buys with his little means
and instills in them story
love
life
and even though we have spent over a decade apart
unable to reconcile sex with no heart
we found platonic love for one another
once the grandkids came

was sex once kept us together
the bed the one place I thought the field was leveled
he loved the fuck but not the cuddle
at least not with me
so he still longed
and I still reached
now both of us searching
hurting
so unintentionally celibate
so late in and
so weary of the game
we both finally see
he no longer tries to lure me back but
he buys me small things
to give each time he sees me
so I can know
that what he gave
so long ago
unrecognizable to me
was love
he buys me books
now that he knows my heart
but mostly he buys me hearts
trinkets
all kinds of hearts
glass
wooden

porcelain
crystal
pendant
hearts he places in my hand
unconcerned about hiding his tears
hearts he finds second hand
and finally
I can thank him for them
rather than complain and
throw them away
even as I no longer have space for them
I've learned to just accept and pass them on and
too often now I find myself
buying trinkets
hearts
talismans
to give to the young girlfriend
of my son
JuanAndrés
Aqua
as he's known to his friends.

DELIVERY

To those who simply ask
why'd you stay
as if endurance
was more shame than complication
I met him when my residence was
southwest cul-de-sac
Roosevelt Park
where you can score anything in a baggie
slept in mama's hand-me-down '78 Ford LTD
gold
like October's leaf carpet end
chill setting in
he had a thick-ass quilt his grandmama made
said *tap my window when you need a place to stay*
my homelessness
meant to last a moment in summer
worked so late yet
short in pay to catch up
on a place just for me
so after work I'd arrive at the park
in time to experience the darkness alone
witches will tell you
there's a reason that hour is their hour for it

but he came at it from the other side
waking as I sought rest

off to work as I fell for the night
or for twenty-two years of my life
attempt at perfection lived twice
four badass kids otherwise
so you tell me

should I have left
first time I reached for keys and
he socked me upside the head
with that sledgehammer fist of his

or when we ran to San Antonio
tried to leave me miles from nowhere
seven months pregnant in the summer sun
couldn't pry me from the wheel
took the keys
so barefoot I ran up from behind with all my might
leapt WWE-like
clotheslined to the broken pavement
K   E   Y   Scattered and instead
I drove us to L.A. where
Amanda was born
my first Mother's Day
socked to the floor
through the glass top of the coffee table
ass up

face down in the shards of
an affair he could no longer hide

or when we ran home where
Angelica was born
then three months into her life
had to leave in the night in an old green Ford LTD
he bought with cash
cocaine kilo stashed
had no idea
'til he had to show me how
to shoot his gun again on the run
to Denver where Ambrosio was born
delivered myself
dad and nurse insisted
it wasn't my time
pushed him forth
pulled him out myself
in his first breath
in his first glance
in his slippery yet curious face
I saw myself
anyway
brought him home
hours old
on the midnight Trailways bus from Denver

or eight years later
when brother manifests brother
JuanAndrés was born of Ambrosio's daily prayer
         for a little brother and
my rebirth
education
ability to finally take his sledgehammer fist
three times to the head
without a flinch
miseducation
my room years later
studying criminal law for the bar exam
he's swinging machete
threatens to chop off my head
go ahead or shut the fuck up I said
not doing this again
the bar's in two weeks
so yeah
I'll quiz on the laws you break on me
Assault
Deadly weapon
Battery
Interference with communication
Kidnapping
Child endangerment

to his credit
became the line
where he finally let us go
alive rather than dead
see there are no short stories
where I'm from so
in simple response to your ignorant why
I reclaimed my time precisely
in the moment
manner
manifested through
blood curse and tears of
twenty-two fucking hard-fought and -won years.

THOSE BLACK PANTIES

it was both
sheer and blind terror that night
as he made his way to turn on the light
so she could find them
on his dark sheet
ugh no blanket to hide behind
underneath
backside
stretch marks
cellulite
might not invite her back if he sees
her cottage cheese
so she must act fast
wipes her ass
with the blue gas-station paper towels he tosses her way as
her hands scramble across the black futon of his bed and then
in a drop to her knees
the floor
the foot of the bed
distracted by beer
smell of head on her lips
not similar but same
though this one's grayed
only the name has changed
her mind shifts back down
to the bulge of her hips

shacked up and hid for so many years
and she will not
cannot
expose them here
to his eyes the way she just has
to the wild blind of his drum-playing hands
as they'd rippedatstrippedatspankedat her ass
now her fumbling hands race
so he doesn't see
they're panties
not lace
not string
but she can't see a thing
and damn those black panties
she wears on nights she thinks she stands a chance
holds onto a laugh that they're practically new and
wishes she knew what to do
or at least the rules on leaving them behind
in such a bind
or what he'd think
on finding them later on tonight
or in the a.m.
bright and early
six o'clock
so he'd said
as he'd tossed her out of his bed

killing her plan to leave before that
but just glad
he makes way for and turns on the bathroom light instead
giving her extra time
yet still not enough light
she screams in her head
still searching the bed
as he rinses and gargles her out of his mouth
swishing with blue Listerine
she can smell as he spits her over and over in the sink
as over and over
she runs her hands through the bed
distracted again
desperate to rinse him away
eyes the Marble Red beer
she'd left on the stand as he'd pull her away to the bed
she has a habit of never finishing
that last warm sip
but if she could just swish with it here
really knowing bottle-bottom beer
is so similar and same in its brine and its shame
in the way the smell still turns her on
ugh
anyway
he shuts off the water
she figures in her head

the number of seconds before he turns and finds her
still bent over the bed
still searching
still naked
awaiting his light
in silhouette he heads her way
soft
clean
she wonders how many like her he's seen
or as of late
have seen him this way and
she still searching the bed
with absolutely no time left
as he brushes by to turn on the bedroom light
she grabs fast
even as she wonders how it will feel she jumps bare-assed
    into her pants
in that leftfootrightfootpullthemupwriggleinzipperpulling
    dance
just as he flips on the switch and
voila
there they are
tucked in the molded pocket
her ass had left in his futon mattress bed
she quickly nabs
shoves in her pocket before he sees

her to the door
without a word said about calling again
shuts off the porch light
before her key even finds the lock in the car door

from there her head engages nothing
but broken white lines that
guide her to her own front door
three in the morning
knocking
fumbling forgotten keys
turns her pockets
sees in the dark where she stands
only tumbling blue paper towel and
black panties in hand.

HEAD HANGOVER

foolhardy really
how after full percolation
contemplation
speculation of three nights fallen
he should finally call Monday night to ask
if I have thoughts on what did or didn't happen between us
    in bed on Friday night
thoughts?! like death-match haiku?
like twenty-second-over-the-three-minute-limit slam version?
expectations of silence instead whisper *give it to me*
fuckin' A I say
sit back
keep it shut till I'm done
ten to one top thoughts on what happened Friday night:

10)   that "wicked how good you kiss" line, really hot, use it a
      lot? well it worked as

9)   I was so taken as to tongue-kiss your recently vomiting
      mouth and you were so drunk as to have me, though
      your regret throbbed worse than your head as you
      repeated again and again "this didn't really happen, this
      didn't really happen, this didn't really happen" as

8)   thirteen years younger than me you have reputation
      to keep, I know those two hundred or so tight young
      hotties you've had and my body won't make the cut as
      two hundred one except maybe in pounds as it consists

of mountainous terrain, wilds of which your
fingers ain't never had to tame but

7) I too have a reputation to keep, in-my-head
divorcée fox stepping out her box, sexpot ready
to rock the world for any cock showing up willing
and naked but suck you as I may choked out for
air and you didn't even let me get you there

6) yeah, okay, so your fingers all twirled up in my hair
while I was down there left me with a bouffant
that scared off your scaredy-cat dog and

5) maybe you placed the pillow over your face to
escape the pathetic attempt at bounce by my
gravitationally challenged tits or

4) maybe you just break girls up into manageable bits
so it never adds up to making love even though

3) you did rub me vigorously enough my pubic hair
might burst into flame or I'd spray out a genie
calling your name granting your prayer to get the
hell out of there and just as orgasm should have
yanked the memory away we passed out and

2) the way we slept, your fingers in your curls and
mine on my clit really, no really, what in the world
did you expect as

1) fucking never in the history of EVER has there
been such a pair of dysfunctional misfits ever so

perfectly matched for the moment
so what do you say
we on again for Friday?

PREY

predator
animal that preys on others
person who does the same
adept ones adapt
deflect suspicion
predator onto prey

like that day we camped
I had just given you head down by the creek
in long grass I hoped you'd roll me in
as I still lay there titties hanging out
instead you stood
tapped
zipped your camouflage cargo pants
tucked in steel-toed boots
pistol within reach of your dominant hand
Bowie knife glared jagged teeth
how dare I believe there's some goddess in me
like there is god in you
spit screams at me
how threatening I am
that I don't understand
how the fuck threatening I am
predator
like when you say she's hotter than me
'cause she swallows more deeply

prey
like when you finally gave
said get on top
immediately you went soft
slapped my left breast so hard
you left handprint bruise
predator
like two nights later
I went with him because my friends watched
he'd stalked me since and from the dance floor
cute and way younger than me with that reputation to keep
desperate for love
he'd kissed me desperately in the shadows
flipped me around face first into the wall
I want your ass
he'd breathed in my ear
but only if you've not recently been with any other men
I laughed in my head
like how the fuck this dude gonna know
I'd not been with anyone new in twenty years
but you
two nights before
invites me for a cruise down the road to his place
real quick he says
he'd left the irrigation running in his alfalfa field
don't wanna flood the field he says

tools hang and clank from the rails of his pickup truck
I'm your handy man
tool box size of a coffin rests in the bed
had to move two others in front so I could climb in
yanks me close
yanks my clothes off
as he steers the private drive to his place
hand already clawed up inside
as he parks in the field
windows down
I drown in the moment
trickle of water
smell of sweet
green
wet
and no one to hear a thing
I realize
as he realizes hand-print bruise on my breast
immediately his hands squeeze my neck
you'd better pray
FUCK ME
I'm gonna have your ass anyway
no one will hear
you said you'd been with no other men
WHORE
WHORES ALWAYS LIE

WOMEN ARE ALL WHORES WHO LIE
so I do
(pray)
with every of my oral skills to get out of that shit
as he shoves my face to his dick
I realize the true danger I'm in
predator
danger is he really ain't got no dick
like not enough to give a hard-on with
toadstool
yet every
tool
known to man
to compensate for it
hoes
sledgehammers
stakes
shovels
rakes
don't even try

prey
lucky day
got him off quick
convinced to just drop me off valet
made way

vomited in the ladies' room sink
scrubbed my tongue with nails of my left hand
all soap and
come back to the room just in time
to be punchline of my friends' joke
who had just rock paper scissors'ed to see
who'd share beds with me and
my "cock breath"
you have no idea I said
as I laid my head
still gagging on that pearly white soap
poor you he had no cock
they said
good thing he had other things to get you off ha
they say

IN NEED of ONE in NEED of a TIT

from what I have come to know
there are four kinds
ones watch from the shadows for that moment you're weak
ones chase hard enough to take you down at the knees
ones recognize they need your scent to attract the next
ones in need of a tit
so goddamned in need of one in need of a tit
available ones
not available enough
only taken ones have balls to approach
taken ones
only want dirty little secret
not-available-enough ones
only want dirty little secret
but not enough
how many fucking lifetimes a woman must resuscitate herself
to find forgiveness
men always forgive the sins of men
but woman's sin is blood

so in goddamned need of one in need of a tit
unafraid to grab hold with both fists and
knead them back to life
desires more than to just kitty-lick around the nipples
but who in sweet relief instinct
wraps his entire mouth around
to swallow so deep

as he'd like to be swallowed in
but another thing I know
takes one with a mighty deep black hole
to want to swallow
fermentation of rejection I've been drowning in
affection I cannot even
give away
can't give what no man is willing to take
can't make you love me if you don't
good thing I know how to float

never got a chance to nourish
sustain life
three kids born unable to latch
one kid that could needed more than I had
one hears how breast food
is best to sustain new life
interactive human magic
mother provides nourishment
child's suckling saliva
speaks back to the mother
of the nutrition it lacks
and the titty reads
and the mama craves what they need her to eat
and the body provides

nobody ever said
in anything I've read
how the titty needs
that knead
that suckle of the teat
to sustain the life of the mother attached
particularly in times of flashback
her dirty little secret
of the one she had sucked from her core
in bits and blood and silence
because the child she already had
set for surgery the following week and already
required all she had
was not her idea
was a cup she'd hoped he'd dash in and save her from
was silence what killed her
nobody ran in to save her from that chair
she couldn't move
no air
no chance to hold at her breast
no chance at a chest to hold her
no air
nor shoulder to anchor in yanks of darkness
swallowing wound of her collapsed star
no shoulder would dare
so remember would be her truth

arrow embedded in scarred-over wound
yank it out
be prepared to bleed
everyday every bit remembered
every bit in black bag
that would be a woman now
a mother
suckling child at her own tit
how many fucking lifetimes a mama must live to
have such shit
forgiven
fucking never so in need one in need of a tit
and you know he could use the
rest there too
for wailing
was what killed him
who didn't know what to do
how to drink
nor how to cry.

NIGHT of the TEAR-DROP

Her godness on the mountaintop
silver flame
Morning Star
Maker of Sunrise
Lady of Ten Thousand Names

Supreme King Maker
Queen of Heaven
Star of the Sea
Sirius
Isis
Iset
Ixchel
Ishtar
Inanna
Astarte
Asherah
Bastet
She Who Gave Birth to Heaven and Earth
Eye of Horus
Mother and son embraced on her lap
one hand cradles his head
the other offers the nipple of life gently between her fingertips

She Who Knows How To Make Right Use of the Heart
She Who Knows the Orphan

Father and son embraced on his lap
one hand cradles his head
the other offers the trigger of death
his fingers gently tighten the vest
too big for his rapidly beating chest
in kisses
in whispers of martyrs and
blazes of white light
he hopes this will be his great moment
for he who fears for his son's welfare
does not seek to save himself from the fires of hell

Oh Lady of Warmth and Fire
Lady of Perfect Love and Perfect Peace
Mistress of Flesh

So small, his hands circle her waist as he tosses her
       to the ground
where he kneels
bows
straddles her fight
folds hands in prayer before thrusting
pinning her
as she fights now for mere breath
teeth rip into her budding breast
she will cry

it hurts
please stop
I swear to God I give just kill me
he'll smash and cover her mouth
hand spattered in blood
he will kneel again when he is done
chants spill from his lips with pride and a burning inside
from breaking this second-class human
girls don't live
girls only survive
to be passed to the next
which is how they are to afford
this life of death
girls do not matter
not mother not daughter

Driven like sheep by the edge
moans loud enough to shake the heavens
we should have all just died together
rather than weather their paradise carved of those
ten thousand words
in this Dark Night whose sun is in its place of yesterday
but his god
his god only dies
his god is only reborn

Lady of Words of Power
Great Lady of Magic
She Who Knows the Widow Spider
kills and gives rebirth

Why is ISIS afraid of girls
for he killed by a girl does not enter his heaven

Most Mighty One
Lady of the Solid Earth
Lady of the Green

Ladies in camouflage
green fatigues
ten thousand sisters embraced on each other's laps
cradling head to cheek
exchanging whispers of insolence and
laughter of the damned
the elders with gentle fingers fix the youngers' hair
fix the grip on rifle stocks
tighten the Kevlar vests already constricting their chests
ISIS they said
will find no fury like woman torn from her home
child torn from her breast
to fight a war she cannot afford not to win
so torn, so she lives

so smile and tell her you love her
cry for her
hug her
make her immortal
remember her
write psalms and songs to her
scream inflection and rhythm in her name

She More Powerful than a Thousand Soldiers
She Who Seeks Justice for the Poor
Alpha and Omega
Lady Breath of Life

I, Isis, am all that has been
that is
or shall be
no mortal man hath ever me unveiled
the fruit which I have brought forth is the Sun

VENUS ROSE

Apparently it's your shore I've always wandered
only place I see my mark
temporary as it may be
seen by only me
only when I look back in time
filled
washed in the foam
Venus rose from this earth of oceans crashing
even before the wind
soul with toes already in the abyss
just let your mind roll on
path of nine
one degree shy of perfection anyway
then there you are
the one
the cool blue I follow from a distance
of no real force of my own
of elemental geometric echoes
of Earth five
Venus six
eleven
perfection
plus one
or two ones
or simply two
I don't know

I don't argue numbers
I can argue anything
ask my dad who rather than smack this insolent
     Catholic girl
simply shook his head
said *ay you can be a lawyer when you get older*
taught from early on to read
reason
argue anything,
write
infinitely divide
if only it was as simple
as times, addition, subtraction of love
hard enough to be Venus in the sky
black as the dark night she was so they said
blemishes
pockmarks of impact
cosmic hits from arrows fired
for being so high above them
so they said
all hoping to be her first
her only
disfigurement
deflection
up close
reflection

embattled
freeze-dried scarred
drop a lit match in black hole of my mouth
I'll flicker smoke from a bottomless fire
that you won't forget me
as eight Earth years
equal thirteen Venus
if only it were simple as love
lust
intellect
chemistry
morality
mortality
but cosmic
molecular
how the fuck do you fight that
universes turn on our dance and
I am terrified
I tried all the ways
all the channels leading in and out
hang
drop
tie the knot
spin the path of the fool
the witch
the orbit

the bard
the goddess
the whore
the swallow
the four
the orbit
the bitch
the sword
the wrist
the three the six the nine
the truth
the fear
is no longer having to fear it
the ever-lapping shore he's ever walked looking for her
      where he left her
Aphrodite lassoed down face-first onto the shore
left for lost bobbing foghorn blows
driftwood carved in licks by mood of your moon
brushed against your leg as you wade and wander
crashed against the rocks of your lighthouse
caught in the ebb there, the orbit
never your favorite poet
I could be your favorite witch
but I suck at math
the kid in me though loves Spirograph
all plastic wheels cogs straight pins colored pens

no artistic bone
but I can create spinning song
thing about magic
you can't have it if you doubt it
no matter that you go
where you go
how long you go
how far you go
who you dance with while you are gone
you'll spin back at least
in a millennium and a half
if we don't meet here
now
in these lifetimes in between
these fly-bys that shred me
the tug
harrowing
yet not enough to draw you back this time around
simply to draw the curve of a petal
like the throat of a swan
like the half of a one on the abalone shore
beautiful they say
they try but cannot quite grasp
the fire and ice heart-driven rose of our dance
your Venus
desire

fire
never get away
equally fucked
ever searching the horizon for that One
end so eternally spectacular anyway
no need to fear it
just turn, water closing around and let this heavenly
       body fly.

MY BLOOD/YOUR BLOOD

Woman
woman left
left lonely
left for not enough love in this world of
touch smell sight taste and sound
as blood flesh and bone
that adorns broken men
you who will die without the love you kill her for being
purple
like her inside
you wear wiped in stripes on your sallow cheeks
her blood like sweat falls to the ground where you leapt
heart pierced
a spear
immediately blood appears
and water
rain sliced of her vein so damned and goddamned
of its natural course in unnatural pain that
you tap and catch with cup of His covenant
serve garnished with spirits and a celery stalk
drawn of her quill
leeched of her well
always bleeding for you
for the life of the flesh is in her blood
He has given it for you to atone for your hells
the spirit
the water

the blood in all her cells
for only love is real
love is the master plan
love is the master's plan
love's where the master plants
these three agree, woman left lonely
when he would die for her
bleed to love her
bleed *to love* her
bleed to love *her* and
she need not look far
she'll use your own words
when she passes you by
sees you wallowing in her blood
says to you in my blood *live*
for worthy are you who take this scroll and open its seal
for you were slain
yet by her blood remain
then you ransomed her
Woman of God
of every tribe
of every language
of every people
of every nation
let's go shed some blood
'cause heaven ain't heaven without it

She will prepare you for blood
as blood shall pursue you
because you did not hate the bloodshed you gave
so be prepared to bleed and
since you have taken all confidences
to enter her holy places
in desecration of dignity
trinity
divinity
for god is Love and
Love is god and
in your self-imposed divine forbearance
you passed Her over
you passed Her by
you passed Her around
you formed Her sin
you sinned Her form
you will suffer for this
as deserved by one who so outraged
His spirit of grace
who has spurned Her
profaned Her blood
by which She was so sanctified
which you so readily sacrifice and
She need not look far
She'll use your own words

for every boot of the tramping warrior in battle tumult and
every garment ever rolled in Her precious blood
will be but burned as fuel for the fire
performing your ritual duties
places only your high priest prays
but not without taking Her blood
which he offers for himself and
for the unintentional sins of his people

yet by this blood spirit indicates
that the way into that holy place
those pearly gates you so crave
not yet even opened
so long as sacrifices are made
that cannot perfect the conscience of that worshipper
regulations on Her body imposed
until the time of reformation
this debate is closed and
for sprinkling Her blood
all over your nations
may grace
peace
spirit
be multiplied unto you
as it is finished
as it is

as I am
the three
for god's sake
I am He.

GIRL WHO WOULD BE KING

girl who would be you
me
girl who would be King
look in the mirror
really look
past your reflection
deep into the unique important magic from the moment
    you first inhaled
purpose
card you were dealt
Empress
Goddess from the moment you bled
though by then
the pimp strategy of the world will begin its attempt
    to fracture you
to zero
to sell you for nothing
to see you bleed self-esteem
to sell you everything
what it doesn't understand is you don't fuck with the universe
know you are the universe
look again
you will never be as beautiful as you are now
young
as you are in this moment in this mirror
divine song

see yourself
beware the boy that says
what makes you beautiful is that you don't know
        that you are
know that you are
TRUTH
stand there
become revolution
own it and
let it go at the same time
as they never intended woman as property owner
only property as you are earth herself
know that someone will always want to claim
        the ground you stand
so, stand
they will scorch you in attempt to save you
plot survey develop subdivide
call you virgin whore dog bitch cunt score witch sin
to get you to give up give in but
each of us is all of them
sooner you embrace their labels sooner they lose propriety
they will never call you home
god
master
jedi
expert

wizard
enough
but you are all of it
the whole of the world
fill it
feel it
shake them off
heal thyself within thyself
they will be offended that you experience heaven there
offenders always offended
you have seen their demon
she is you
as is their hell
sit in their construction of you where those demons howl
llorona
face her
take her
swallow
digest
release her shame one howl at a time
won't be none their hell when you're done
don't you know?
even the son of War and Love is Love
honey-spun divinity unto and of yourself
slithering belly upon the ground
into golden stars underneath your own feet

hissed for your own writhing hair
pillar of salt demons
disturb their universe
dare to feel
when you feel you live
when you live you defy their everyday deaths
tap that power even if it is just getting out of bed
        to face yourself again
even if your superpower is darkness itself
as there murmur forgotten burials of
ancestors planted in sparks that big bang generations
universes
as you are
as I AM
life and love itself
in this moment
in this banging galaxy in the mirror.

BUFFALO SOLDIER
(for Ahjani)

Meanwhile, in daylight on the dark side
in a world full of weeping
yet so full of song
where every footfall's a prayer
appears
approaches in white
adobe girl floated down from stars
barefooted across the plains
snakes and wolves at her feet
she of so many names and yet
anybody's baby
indigenous girl
thoughts dance behind her flashing eyes
where few could look
and those who dared
saw pools of perfect blackness
themselves
as they really were
naked and revealed.
When she spoke at last
her voice the song of waters upon rocks
cracked
choked
oozing black serpent spew
from being slit gullet to womb
so deep it dislodged the electric charge of her beating heart

millions of years to bury what was best left buried
a million gallons of pick-your-poison
slow killing all it touches
young mothers suckle babies
with milk of breasts fed from
wells and creeks where their cattle and sheep drink
where since the beginning poison has leached and leaked
A MILLION GALLONS OF RADIOACTIVE WASTE
a million gallons of oil they will actually claim
a million buffalo slaughtered for show
a million smallpox blankets for the cold
a million gallons of whiskey for your vote
a million voters purged from the rolls
a million children ripped from their homes
          and their tongues from their throats
a million daughters right now being bought raped
          and sold
a million more murdered and missing and
erasure of
their trail of tears
leaves them cold
a million unmarked graves
planted in fields of unrequited hate
where she does not even count
enough to be counted.

Oh but she counts
is all that counts
and she is counting down and

oh when the true west wind blows
her name remembered
lonely drum songs burnt across the plain
beware the rain that comes
once his lament for her has been sung.

Oh girl every time I see you
you put a smile on my face
takes me to this beautiful place
oh how I wish that you were mine
I'd be happy all the time

You see her friends are all warriors now
so take it slow.
Wait for them to ask you who you know
don't make any sudden moves
you don't know the medicines they use.
She'll stretch out her arms
palms facing the sun and know the direction from which
      her enemies come
binding unbinding of her long blowing mane
whirling cloud of wind hail lightning appears in her name

unleashed
the wrath of the love of a million sons.
No watershed safe.
No artery escapes.
You're best to hunker down son
as it's gonna be a hard, hard rain.

PISTOLERA

Pistolera brushes fingers up his spine
el de camisa negra quien tiembla d'ella
who like the others
would take her
shake her
break her if he could
pendejo
tampoco se atreba aprobarse de su arroz
as well he warns his bros y ellos tambien
tirandole le la culpa al embruja y mintiéndoses repentes
que entre ella no puede ver
tentacíon
miel virgen
amerce
y ella nomás sirena del río
tomando sol sin pena
como si no fuera su aroma, risita, idioma
que los tiene veniendo cerquitas, siguentes
atrallente con su canto
y ay pero su canto
Oshun sonriente
o a veces soplando aguardiente de botella de vidrio azul
but for now
she brushes fingers up his spine simply checking his level
        of wired
so tired of lip service

lyin' eyes
unchecked heat
promise of meat and
fuck you
I love you
she tosses to tongues of sage and lavender jones
purple dreams she breaks with the
malas, hociconas, jotos, hijos de la chíngada
that grace her table and
chant myth and
weave doctorates and
feed laughter to the efforts of men in their lives
who are looking for some trouble tonight
it's alright
her fight she takes down to Ray's Automotive on the corner
where they sing and
play Elvis, mariachi and Jesus
between lube jobs
atrallente con su canto
y ay, pero su canto
y ellos tambien tirandole culpa al embruja
y ella nomás Oshun sonriente o a veces
soplando aguardiente de botella de vidrio azul
from which she now chugs and passes to
the cabrónas, hociconas, cochinas, hijitas y gramitas
that grace her table

and take it con HOWWWL
sin vaso sal o limón cabrón
feeding laughter to the efforts that men in their lives give
to feed between lips
bits of cock or
metal like lleguas spur-kicked
broke
ridden
then bold-face lie
deny
each time they are bucked off
fucked off
crumbled into an abalone concha she lifts to her whispers
        of fire
smoke shadows dance upon her piel de cobre
ojos cerrados
oro reflejado
humo emindando de a plumas adornando su cabello negro
breathe breath blow blue sparks swirl
suspire pendejos que bailan en el humo como de a
balas tiradas de
las pistolas de las abuelas
que ajúan, cabrónes
desagradecidos
que se dan vuelta y luego
desaparecidos

en el humo copal
que'ole a accordion y guitarra
que lloran de pecho abierta desde su mesa
un canto que hace temblar
desde su mesa
a donde unos llegan y otros se van
like somebody she used to know
don't it always seem to go
paloma negra
que te irás en silencio de su cantar
y vacuidad de su amar
y dios te de fuerza que te mueres
y el de camisa negra espiando por la ventana
persigniandóse
rezongándole a la Virgen
habizandoles a todos los bros que se cuiden
para que nadie mas que el la mire
admire
desde'l abajo de la botella

porque entre ella allí se fue la neighborhood
faces changed so you don't know them
streaks dyed dark enough to never be huera again
la con quien el movida maker ups the ante
a la quien le toquo a puerta la revoluccíon
pero que cabrón

too much to ask for one who comes from where
    she comes from
deep, eye to eye y ay
pero su canto
deja sombra en todas las que despues el atoqua
make out like it never happened
like she was nothing
but she don't even need your love so
respira de ese humo amargo de su adiós
porque honey, you met your match tonight
saco lla los clavos de su penar
para mano a mano luchar
el dicho y el hecho
hijos de la chingada
porque she just can't… wait…
won't care
what that loaded gun there
is for
no more.

SERÁS TU, CAPITÁN
(SUPREME CHIEF of the REVOLUTIONARY
MOVEMENT of the SOUTH)

That night
Zapata washed my feet
handlebar whiskers scratch the itch between my legs like
myth
reflected in the moon on the mesa
like tongue of silver sage reaching as he rides and rides
     underneath
     the moon's watchful breath
rides and rides all night in great quicksilver strides
to the end of the night of a thousand five hundred years
calor de aliente, respiras caliente
wings of exhale lead the way
smell of earth and dirt disturbed into flight by those four legs
     forged in steel like
hands carved from the dust that flies to the beat of the earth
this land belongs to those who work it with their hands
mi campesino
where it was law that money ruled all
you took it back
gave it back
plowed fields and acequias
planted schools and campesino credit unions
self-ruling
communitarian
democracy
un pueblo unido

the politic of confidence always incites betrayal
"the city is full of sidewalks" you say
"and I keep falling off them"
pay no mind to that
what with twenty thousand soldiers you overthrew
       the capital Capitán
not in rape and plunder
but thirst and hunger
knocking door to door asking for food and water
trai'me ese hambre commandánte
y tu sed te injusticia
que te esperan mis botas
a pie, y sobre el llano te llama mi llanto
y te dibujare con mi canto
y serás tu, Zapata
quien eschucho tocandome en la mañanita
come to me
Supreme Chief of the Revolutionary Movement
       of the South
fly home like falcon
roost in my mouth
yet remain free as we understand the battle is left at the door
enter
and on my knees I will remove your boots
and the shame of your tears
as you overthrew the capital
so you do now with me

here
as has always been my wish
eye to eye
ojo a ojo
frente a frente
raíces enredandose
jamás seremos vencidos
never again to be defeated
the smell of earth and death disturbed into flight by our
four legs forged in steel like
hands carved from the dust that flies to the beat of the earth as
your eyes understand my fight and
your hands recover my lands
as promised a time of truth and justice
now rest
face buried in my chest
inhaling sweat and tears from my breast
lost in my blood
hint of copper on your lips
kiss me
I will finally find homeland
Atzlán
in the aura of your crown
magic from which others turn and run yet
I stand ground and call
oleme
in smoke of your body riddled with bullets

fired from every of their rifles
until emptied
escúchame
in the laughter of fifty thousand pesos
besos del traidor
MATENLO
then in the footsteps of the burro that carries you home
    to Cuautla
for only half the bounty
your body displayed
photographed as proof of your non-existence
so why did the one have to die
for you to arrive
as between the two
who is truth
as still your horse can be seen
prancing
galloping
bucking
reflecting silver underneath the sun
even as the time for talk is done
nothing but to await your hoof beat
you need but reach your arm for my leap
we'll raise dust from this place
silver-tongued sages reaching
as you and I ride away.

CAPTAIN

I fantasize of you fantasizing of me
of your nose catches notes of my hair on hiccups of wind
of your lips part and eyes light
on the thought of how you took me from behind
in the dark of my office that night
bathed in the monitor screen's blue essence
transcribed pain
I was representative of a wrongful death claim
(what is it about death
make fucking the cure)
you and I
both done in
empty
and yet you'd walked over to see me
four blocks in the rain

I hold your face
remove your cap
lap that drips from the warm that wisps from your crown
down your furrowed brow
breaks for the peak of your cheekbone
plinkoed through your whiskers
nectar to the desert of my tongue
salted by your eagerness to enter my mouth which
slides so easily over you
into you

can't believe this is happening
yank and toss my top
you my bra and then
my cute red skirt you were so happy to see me in
oblivious to my hips
aware of every prayer on my lips
trembles and drops to the tile ahead of your hands
already on deck
stroll the cameo of my neck
like breath caress my vessel my curves
my silhouette my breasts my breath arrest
 as your fingers press down the edge of my
chest my chocolate brown puckered nipples
waiting erect your hands running smoothly
down and smoothly back as you slide the
panties down off my ass hands smoothly
down smoothly back again past my now
tingling tits as my hips you grasp and
rotate bow to ass one-eighty like
captain of the ship like ooh
back into your hips like
you're thick like

your long fingers first
land footprint on my shore
my shimmer where ghost waves
mark the ebb and flow of my core
then climb to twirl and tuck my hair up
to smudge your nose from ear to ear on
sea salt course a millennium planned and yet
your lips rumble subway tracks on the ridge of my back
you continue to glide past sides of my ass,
smoothly down and smoothly back and I arch
my chest thrumming breasts erect, your fingers
strumming over my nips that sing to every ripple
on the tips that finally hit then meet in between
that strum the flesh that drums the bones that
wind the staircase to my throat your palms
cup, swirl like you're thick like a boa glide
over my shoulder slithering down my
spine tickling to my quivering
behind where you suddenly
smack a cheek

your hand print read

But I'm Libra I must've said
you can't do to one
what you don't do to the other

wait

palpitate

salivate

heart race

you bend me all the way onto my glass top
desk where many a man's fantasy about to
be now laid to rest as I push piles of papers
and files to the floor as my nipples now
pressed to the glass
as you see me
ass
as you gaze me
ass
as like never
ass

steam wisps my hands to the glass
as yours cup and pat

as I
gasp and
pant and
wait for the sting
pray for it
trembling
I won't
breathe
I won't be
afraid of what you see
stretched
opened wide
in bated breath
elated inside
wait
sting
pray
you step back and say
grrrl
you bent over
waiting for me like that

is the hottest thing I've ever seen...

There you have it, crone.
Accept your goddamned crown.

GOOD GODDESS SOUL FUCK

I believe what you seek is
a good goddess soul fuck
so unlike the orifice fuck of simply afraid of
soft
lost in
body
hair
musk
surrender your divine to the conscience of pleasure
too often sufficed instead with a full Brazilian
bled paid sex effort already made and for this
we have given up lips
the kiss
the dripping honey wine suckling of sweet luscious locked
      in surrender of
tongue reading lips sucking tongue
of just read your body baby from dusk to dawn
of only the first one
open mouth communion
open the mind and
you open the body
redefine the mind fuck of sterile
no wonder there is no feral to lure
to keep you there
to drink like a cup off your lip hair
repulsed instead by the very scents that defy

those tragic secret deaths
tuft where arm meets chest
moist creamy under breast
crevice where leg meets hair and
arroyos of life that flow through there
like nard and myrrh
anoint the underneaths of souls and feet that stand
      the very beat
between breath and rest and
dressed and rapt in hair of miss red vessel Magdalene
with tears of joy oils to anoint the violet of your head
rejected again and again instead for
dying unaware
fear worn to bed
she only feels his
part by part rejection
on close inspection
bears what he needs
glossy and sleek
simply taking
taking her
taking it
no connection
other than where orifice meets erection
so blind to the crime we are dying without love
no Oshun flicker of orange gold letting go indigo reflection

exquisite inner genuflect of
cosmos blind to the way the lights fall
where giving yourself to me is never wrong
that place we were conceived
healed in green
suckled
held
adored
crash that place
between inhale and ecstasy
between fires gone wild and
ebb and flow dissolve in sea of accretion
mighty Aphrodite I'm capsizing
Yemaya waves rising and rising
in silvery slick secretion beyond wild desire and
fearless Lillith abandon
angel described as lust
Bast Pasht pussy passion uterus
nipples and nebulae pursing
moaning
sweet cursing
as uterus laps head
strokes clit
licks quivering dripping balls
throats hum
mouths opened wide

didn't I blow your mind this second time
Inanna's blue moon purple rain pearl vulva honey well
    cunt throbbing
swallowing gravity
deep space
time
unlock you draw you in imagine
divine cusp of intoxication
I can just stay here inside you and drink as
that leap that will set you free
have you see
and at last be seen
on the verge of a third
letting go in nights in white satin
electric yellow abandon
take my hand as the sun descends and
tell me something good
desirous hunger
the fire whirling swirling astral chemistry of
no longer knowing who is god/child/top/bottom/
    penis/nipple/mother/daddy/dragon/saint
plunging
penetrating
tantric
transcendent
scorching

yearning
burning
squirting soul juice
pussy mused
cock induced alchemy
elliptic
clit
ecliptic
clit
orgasmic
bucking
fucking grinding
clit
touch me now touch me now touch me
aveMariapurisima
goodnightEireen
oh my fucking goddddddddyyeesssssss
event horizon bang
set you free
you see?
good god
what you need is a soul fuck.

ABOUT the AUTHOR

Anna C. Martinez is a mother, grandmother, performance/competitive/slam poet, and civil rights attorney. Born in Los Angeles at the height of its civil rights movements, she was then raised from school age in Española, New Mexico. She is the in-house poet at Las Pistoleras Instituto Cultural de Arte in Taos and has held titles as ABQ Chicano/a City Slam Champ, XXX Haiku City Champ, and 2019 City Slam Champ for team Mindwell Slam. She is also on the board of directors for Burque Revolt Poetry Slam and opens her home for free to touring poets. She lives in Albuquerque.

CASA URRACA PRESS

Casa Urraca Press publishes creative nonfiction, poetry, photography, and other works by authors we believe in. New Mexico and the US Southwest are rich in creative and literary talent, and the rest of the world deserves to experience our perspectives. So we champion books that belong in the conversation—books with the power, compassion, and variety to bring very different people closer together.

We are proudly centered in the high desert somewhere near Abiquiu, New Mexico. Visit us at casaurracapress.com for exquisite editions of our books and to register for workshops with our authors.

CPSIA information can be obtained
at www.ICGtesting.com
Printed in the USA
LVHW010035310322
714641LV00003B/9